SUCCESS WITH CLEMATIS

SUCCESS WITH CLEMATIS

by

J. FISK

With a Foreword by ROWLAND JACKMAN

THE GARDEN BOOK CLUB
121 CHARING CROSS ROAD, LONDON WC2

This edition by arrangement
with Thomas Nelson and Sons Ltd

Printed in Great Britain by
Thomas Nelson (Printers) Ltd, London and Edinburgh

CONTENTS

FOREWORD

Mr Fisk tells us that this book is written ' mainly for the amateur gardener ', and how interestingly he has written it, and with what authority, based on practical experience !

As a man devoted to his subject, and one who has specialised professionally in Clematis to the exclusion of all other plants, he has drawn on his knowledge in a way, that a beginner can fill his garden with colour and beauty, and yet a man of experience will gain something new.

It is abundantly clear from reading this book that the uses of Clematis are many, but there is a very real danger that in the new modern garden a great opportunity is being lost. I refer to the craze of the builder for concreting right round the house and right up to the walls, which deprives the owner of a garden asset of value. May I make a plea for a fresh approach to this subject, so that the ' Queen of Climbers ', and wall plants in general, may be used to the fullest advantage ? That is where a book like *Success with Clematis* can make all the difference.

ROWLAND JACKMAN

INTRODUCTION

CLEMATIS—loveliest of all climbing plants, the Queen of Climbers—are easy to grow.

The descriptive part of this statement will be generally agreed upon by all, but the fact that they are easy to grow will not be accepted by everyone. Furious arguments will rage between those whose gardens are filled with masses of clematis in all varieties, and those unhappy people who ' just can't grow them '.

There is no real reason why they should not thrive for anyone. Providing we look after the plants during their first year of life, and obey a few simple rules, they should live for a great number of years, filling the garden all spring, summer and autumn with their magnificent blooms in their many diverse forms and colours. From the tiny star-like white *C. flammula* to the huge exotic lavender-blue ' William Kennett ', over eight inches across, and no matter how small or how large, all clematis flowers are elegant and graceful. Their colours range through all the blues, mauves, purples and pinks. Wine-red, white and yellow are also there, and some have exotic-looking stripes down the centre of each sepal. The word ' sepal ' is correct, as clematis have no real petals. All these colours blend naturally with other flowers, none of them being harsh or glaring. They are extremely hardy and, with a little care, will grow anywhere in the British Isles.

The trouble is that clematis are not often given that little extra bit of care during their first season. Chrysanthemum devotees spend hours on staking, tying and disbudding their precious plants. Orchid growers are even more fussy, going to great lengths to see that their favourites have all they want—and all they rightly deserve. Clematis, on the other hand, are usually planted in a hurry in the cold and foggy autumn and forgotten about until the following summer.

The nurseryman is probably a little to blame, as clematis are often described as ' hardy '. Of course they are, as hardy as the British oak, but this emphasis on the word ' hardy ' has unfortunate results. The average gardener assumes from this description that the plants will need no looking after at all, so they are usually planted quite casually and left to look after themselves. The plants are usually only one year old with very thin and frail-looking stems which often succumb to the unequal struggle against cats, dogs, neglect or the enthusiastic gardener who hoes neatly through the stem below ground level. A little extra time spent on them during the first year, a little protection round that frail-looking stem, such as a cylinder of wire netting, correct pruning and feeding will ensure that the plant gets off to a good start. In future years it can be left unattended for months on end, but at the same time repaying a hundredfold those first few hours of attention.

The sight of one of the Jackmanii varieties, dripping with royal purple all the summer over some cottage porch, also strengthens the idea that all you have to do is to ' bung 'em in ', and then before you know where you are you will have an enchanting mantle over the front door. I think that the reason these ' cottage porch ' plants thrive and bloom so well, with apparently no attention, is the fact that they are invariably situated on old cottages which have plenty of lime in the foundations. Clematis are lime-loving plants and so take naturally to such a position. Another reason is that in cottage gardens there is usually plenty of shade for the roots, such as catmint, lily of the valley and other low-growing plants, also brick paths or crazy paving, which give the cool and moist root run that is so essential.

INTRODUCTION

Clematis can be grown quite successfully in town and country alike, and there are many fine specimens to be seen in London and other big cities. The not-so-vigorous varieties are ideal for town gardens, such as ' Nelly Moser ', ' The President ', ' Miss Bateman ' and ' Lasurstern '. They will not need the space that the Montana varieties do, for instance, and neither will they need any pruning.

Clematis lovers should get the advice of a reputable nursery-man who *grows his own plants*, and do make sure they are pot-grown. Many nurseries buy in their clematis and know little about them. There are several nurseries that will give you expert advice on the best varieties for your locality, and a list of them can be obtained from any good gardening paper. Some varieties *are* ' not so easy ', so for a start the beginner should try some of the well-tried and faithful sorts that will not let him down. The small-flowering species are really tough and reliable, and the Montana group will grow anywhere, even on north walls. Their star-shaped flowers in varying shades of white and pink smother the rope-like branches during May and June, and they need no pruning. Late-flowering species are also trouble-free and can be relied upon to give a generous show from July to October. They include the yellow lantern-shaped *C. tangutica*, also the various shades of purple, pink and white of the Viticella group. Hard pruning with all late-flowering varieties is the golden rule. They grow so quickly during the early summer that they are at the top of the pergola or house again by mid-summer.

The easiest of all the large-flowering hybrids is undoubtedly the Jackmanii group. These have medium-sized flowers, but masses of them. Purple ' Jackmanii ' and ' Gipsy Queen ', pink ' Comtesse de Bouchard ' and ' Hagley Hybrid ', red ' Madame Édouard André ' and blue ' Perle d'Azur ' are all easy to grow and can be relied upon to give a glorious display all the summer. They all need cutting back hard every year in February, but apart from that they are quite easy to manage.

The huge exotic blooms are the ones that attract so much attention in the garden, and the following varieties are the hardiest and easiest for the beginner.

'Nelly Moser', with her pale-mauve-pink flowers, each sepal splashed with a carmine bar (she will sometimes take a year or two to get settled, but after that she will give a magnificent show every May and June) ; 'The President', with its purple-blue flowers and excellent habit of flowering almost non-stop from May to September ; white 'Henryi' and 'Madame le Coultre', with their enormous plate-like flowers of great distinction ; lavender-blue 'Mrs Cholmondeley', another non-stop bloomer ; and 'William Kennett', with its huge rich flowers in midsummer. All these need little pruning beyond the trimming-back of dead ends in February, and they are well-tried and reliable varieties.

This book is mainly written for amateur gardeners, many of whom long to grow these fascinating climbers, but who are so often put off by tales of clematis being difficult and temperamental. By following the few simple rules of pruning and cultural advice I have given, the would-be clematis grower will find that they are not so difficult after all, that they are the most rewarding of all our climbing plants and that no garden, however small, is complete without some of its walls, fences and shrubs covered with clematis.

SUCCESS WITH CLEMATIS

ONE : PLANTING

CLEMATIS will grow in practically any soil, but if we want the best results it is as well to do the job properly and give them a really good start in life. The plants are grown in pots in the nursery, usually in the four-and-a-half-inch size commonly known in the trade as ' Long Toms '. The soil in these Long Toms is, of course, something a little bit special, and to put the plant straight into the ordinary soil in the garden is asking a bit too much. Some extra work now will be repaid handsomely in the following years, and the reward will be well worth the trouble taken.

Clematis like a deep root run, so we must break up the soil to at least eighteen inches, deeper if possible. It is also a good idea, if the garden soil is poor, to mix in some John Innes Compost. Peat or leaf soil is also a useful commodity if obtainable, and of course some manure is essential, as clematis are gross feeders. If the farm-yard variety is not available, hop manure can be used. Bone-meal is also a good fertiliser for these plants : a handful of this, scattered round each plant in the autumn and worked in, will be very beneficial.

Clematis like good drainage, so if the soil needs this, place some broken brick, mortar rubble or broken pots at the bottom of the hole—anything that will drain the immediate area around the roots. Although clematis like good drainage, however, this does not mean that they like a dry soil ; in fact, quite the reverse is the case. They belong to the Ranunculaceae family, of which the buttercup is a member, and this gives us a clue to the likes of the clematis—a moist but well-drained soil.

If we are planting against a wall (a notoriously dry spot), we must keep this in mind, and it is wise to plant a foot or two away from the wall. We can always train the plant back on trellis or wire, or lay a certain amount of the stem under the soil. Pegging the stem down to the ground between the roots and the wall is a good idea. Roots will form on this laid-in or pegged-down stem, and there will also be buds on it in case it should get accidentally broken at any time.

Our hole, then, should be about two feet deep, and if possible two feet square, the bottom three or four inches covered with broken-brick rubble or similar drainage, and on top of this a good layer of farm-yard or hop manure. Our excavated soil should have been either replaced with some good loam, or mixed with John Innes Compost, two ounces of bone-meal to the square yard should have been added, and a few spadefuls of soil placed in the hole. We are now ready, then, to plant our clematis.

When planting against a wall, fix trellis or wire before planting —details of supports will be found in the chapter on training. If your plants are sent by rail or post, unpack them carefully, and if they seem at all dry give them a good soaking, leaving them in a pail of water for an hour or two to become thoroughly wet. Plants are often sent out in paper pots, and it is quite a simple matter to tear this off without disturbing the ball of soil (always buy plants that are pot-grown). If your plant is still in its clay pot, however, it can be knocked out quite easily by holding the pot in one hand, then spreading the fingers of the other hand over the top of the soil in the pot, so that the plant with its cane is in between the second and third fingers, the thumb helping to hold the side of the pot. Turn the whole thing upside down, remembering to allow for the cane, gently tap the edge of the pot (now upside down) on to something solid—the handle of the spade for instance—and you will find that the ball of soil will gently slip out into the hand and the pot can be removed with the free hand. We hear of the various methods of planting, ' plant at pot level ', ' plant on a slight mound ', etc., but I have found that it is better to plant a little deeper than the pot level ; roots will always form on the portion of the stem under the ground, to the plant's advantage.

Place your plant carefully on the soil at the bottom of the hole, leaving the cane still in position, and gently fill in, making the soil firm by treading round the plant.

When planting in the autumn or spring, the roots, which often curl round and round the bottom of the pot, can be gently disentangled. This will take a little time and patience, but it helps the plant to spread its roots evenly in the ground. Clematis can, nevertheless, be planted at any time of the year, so if the plant is obtained from the nursery or a garden shop in the summer, it is safest not to disturb the roots at all.

Your soil may be hot and sandy ; in this case, try to incorporate as much moisture-retaining humus as possible—lashings of manure, peat or leaf-soil will help. Your soil may, on the other hand, be heavy clay and difficult to drain. If it is impossible to obtain drainage by brick rubble underneath the plant, try the idea of ring-culture, which is so popular with tomato growers. The plant is grown in a large pot about twelve inches in diameter with no bottom. Filled with good soil, the clematis is planted in this receptacle, standing on its permanent site. The roots will then fill the pot and go down through the open bottom into the heavy clay—which could have been lightened with peat and sand and some manure, buried a foot below. The plant will become established in its pot of good soil, with no fear of being water-logged, and when its strong roots are firmly established below, you will find that the result will be a plant of extraordinary vigour. The pot should be kept well watered during the first year until the plant is firmly established. One could also use a tub with no bottom ; or better still, build a little brick square about eighteen inches high which would retain the moisture more effectively.

The cane, which should have been left, helps to support the plant during the winter, and it can be tied securely to the trellis or wire frame, which is to support the clematis until the spring, when it can be removed as the first pruning takes place.

The stem of a clematis is at this stage very fragile, and so it is a good idea to place a cylinder of wire netting round the base of the plant about a foot high and let into the soil an inch or two. Two or three small canes will support it and hold it in position until the plant is established.

Clematis which grow wild will be found with roots well hidden at the bottom of a hedge, in competition with many other plants. This proves that they do best when grown with other plants—shrubs, roses, etc.—especially when the host can give the desired protection from the sun. A hot dry soil is fatal to clematis, so we must imitate nature and provide a cool moist root run. Bedding plants, rock-garden plants or small shrubs can be used to plant in front of and around the clematis, or stone slabs, tiles and crazy paving, for underneath these it is always cool and moist. Pebbles scattered thickly round the base of the plant are also very effective—the rain can soak through, and they look neat and tidy. I have even seen sacking stretched incongruously but effectively over the roots ; anything to provide that essential shade.

Many modern houses are surrounded by concrete, but if you can break a small hole through, close to the wall, this will be the ideal situation for a clematis. The hole need only be very small, six inches long by four inches wide, but deep enough to get some manure and good soil in, and the plant itself. Some of the best plants I have ever seen appear to grow out of the concrete. They love the cool moist earth below, and once the plant is established there will be no worries about its drying out.

When planting, it is a good idea to sink a four-inch or five-inch pot beside each plant, so that the top of the pot is level with the soil. Through the drainage hole in this pot we can water our plants very simply without wasting it on the surface of the soil. The water will get down to the roots quickly, where it is wanted, and liquid manure can also be given through this pot during the summer. If a sunken pot by each plant looks out of place, a small tile can be placed on the top, which can be lifted each time we water the plant.

Our clematis is now well and truly planted, and we must make sure that we have provided it with something on which to climb gracefully. This is dealt with in the chapter devoted to training, but first of all we must make sure that the plant is pruned and looked after properly during its most important first year of life.

TWO : THE FIRST YEAR

Assuming that your clematis was planted during the autumn, then nothing will need to be done during the winter. The plant can be given a top dressing of manure at the time of planting, and this should be spread round the stem of the plant to about a foot each way. A good thick layer (one could also use compost or hop manure) will help to feed the plant during the winter, and at the same time give it a certain amount of protection. Some of my friends empty their tea leaves round the roots of the plant ; whether there is any goodness in them I hesitate to say, but the plants so treated seem to thrive on their ' tea leaf ' mulch. The time for the first pruning will be in February or early March, depending on the weather, but as clematis start to shoot quite early in the year, the sooner it is done the better. Spring-planted clematis can be pruned back when planting. All hybrids—large-flowering varieties, that is—and late-flowering species (small-flowering varieties) need cutting down, the first spring after planting. The only varieties that do not need this are the early-flowering species, *C. alpina*, *C. armandii*, *C. macropetala*, *C. montana* and their varieties. These can be cut back if desired, but as they will branch out and make good plants if left alone, there is no need for this pruning. But for all the other varieties, the Florida, Lanuginosa, Patens and Viticella groups, do please be ruthless, the first February. You may see some lovely plump buds at the top of the cane, but shut your eyes to these and snip off the stem well below, down to a few inches if possible. You will see the buds forming on the stem at the base—not so forward as the top ones, but buds that will make the well-trained plant of the future. Cut down to just above this pair of buds, with a sharp knife, as close to them as possible, and remove the cane that has been supporting the rest of the plant, unless it is needed for training to the trellis or wire frame on the wall. A dressing of sulphate of potash can be given in March. This fertiliser is ideal for clematis ; it promotes strong growth, good colour in the foliage and flower, and, most important of all, disease resistance. It can be used two or three times during the summer and is very beneficial to the plant. The amount to give is two ounces to a square yard. Sprinkle the powder round the plant and water well in.

During March and April the young plant will begin to shoot. Two strong shoots should develop from the two buds we have cut our clematis down to, but more often than not one of these buds will remain dormant and only one shoot will appear. When this shoot—or the pair, if they both break—are about six to nine inches long, and have a pair of leaf buds on them, cut back to these buds. This will sometimes mean just nipping out the growing tip as one would with chrysanthemums, and the object is just the same : to make the plant break and become nice and bushy at the base, the foundation of a well-grown, well-furnished plant. This process should be repeated two or three times during the first growing season. Every shoot that appears should be stopped after it has made a strong start of about a foot. Clematis do not mind being stopped or pruned in the least, and it all helps to get that well-grown plant, so there is no need to despair if one accidentally breaks off a lovely strong shoot, or the wind batters the plant ; nature will soon send out more shoots to give us a fine specimen plant for the future.

Another most important and vital reason for this continued ' stopping ' during the first year is that this hard pruning wards off the dreaded mystery complaint of clematis known as Clematis

Wilt. When this disease does attack, it is in the first year or two of the life of a clematis. Rarely if ever does a well-established plant suffer from this terror, and even if it does occur, a plant that has been well furnished with strong shoots in its first year will be capable of resisting such an attack.

Many clematis die during their first year for want of this pruning ; the collapse is more often than not caused by allowing too much top growth. The roots are unable to support this, and so many a plant fails before it has had a chance. So remember : during the first spring and summer, prune hard and prune often. Your reward will come.

We have discovered that clematis are moisture lovers, and this aspect must be kept in mind during the first year. Clematis hate being dry at the root, and here is another reason for several failures early in life. Give them a good soaking once a week, a bucketful, rain or no rain. If there is good drainage, you cannot over-water clematis, and by a wall this is most important. A tablespoonful of one of the proprietary liquid manures to each bucket of water will help to feed as well as water your plant. Once they become established they will get enough moisture— in the British climate anyway.

Your plant should be well established by July. After this month no further pruning should be done, and with a little bit of luck you will get a few flowers on the young wood in September.

After the first year follow the pruning directions in the next chapter and give your plant an annual mulching of manure or compost in the autumn (bone-meal is a very good top dressing at this time, two ounces to the square yard), and in the spring that all-important two-ounce dressing of sulphate of potash. Your plant will have had a good start in life and you should have a fine display of magnificent blooms the following year.

8

THE FIRST YEAR

With one-year-old plants we must have a little patience ; it takes at least two years to get a plant really established, and sometimes more. Most nurseries sell only young plants, and so we must not expect a mass of bloom for the first year or two ; our plant will need this time to get itself settled in. It may be possible to obtain two- or three-year-old plants in large pots, but these are difficult to find and much more expensive. If, however, you are lucky enough to find them, it will save at least a year of waiting, and you will get your display immediately.

THREE : TRAINING

As it grows in the wild, we see C. *vitalba*, the ' Old Man's Beard '
or 'Traveller's Joy', covering our hedges with masses of attractive
feathery grey seed heads in the autumn. The roots of the plant,
if they can be traced down through the tangle of growth, are
usually found to be deep in the shelter of the hedge, well away
from the sun, the shoots climbing through the hedge to the light.
There, on the tops of hedges, trees and bushes we find the small
greenish-white flowers in August followed by a billowy mass of
seed heads in the autumn, a most useful decoration for harvest
festivals, and for all floral arrangements during the winter. Here,
then, is the ideal method for training *our* clematis. The large-
flowering varieties are just as suitable for growing on shrubs and
bushes as the small-flowering varieties, and what an exciting
method this can be ! Most flowering shrubs show themselves
off in June, and are a little dull and uninteresting during the rest
of the season. With clematis we have an opportunity of prolonging that flowering season with something quite out of the ordinary.
Just imagine a lilac bush suddenly bursting into blossom again in
July with huge exotic blooms of the white ' Henryi ', or
throughout the whole summer with masses of purple ' Jackmanii '
blooms ! These clematis will do no harm to their hosts, and
if one uses the Jackmanii and Viticella varieties they can be
pruned down to the ground in the autumn or early spring.
By the time they reach the top of the shrub, the flowering
time of the host will have come and gone, leaving the graceful
guest to take over for the rest of the season. I know of
one lady who has a garden of labour-saving shrubs ; every

shrub has a clematis, and her garden is a joy from spring until late autumn.

Planting next to a shrub calls for a little extra care. Plant a foot or two away from the main stem, on the shady side, for we must make sure the clematis will receive sufficient nourishment and that the greedy bush will not starve our plant. A good top dressing every autumn and spring round the clematis will ensure that this does not happen, and the two ounces of sulphate of potash in the spring, repeated in early summer, will keep the clematis full of flower and vigour. Almost any type of shrub can be used for this treatment—the natural way of clematis-growing : even tall trees can have an extra beauty added to them by planting a Montana type to ramble at will over them. A holly tree with its dark-green foliage is an excellent foil for the white or pink C. *montana*. The whole tree dripping with these dainty flowers in the early summer is a delightful picture. I have seen the C. *montana* climbing ash and elm trees forty or fifty feet high, with the waterfall of colour in May and June an amazing sight. They need no pruning, of course, and when the plant has reached its summit the many shoots with their myriad flowers descend in a charming manner to give this living-waterfall effect every year.

Clematis climb by twining their leaves tightly round anything available ; one has only to provide the support and the plant will do the rest. So if we wish to grow them on a wall of the house, on a pillar or porch, we must provide the necessary means for them to climb on. Trellis fixed to the wall is an excellent method, but if we wish to have the support as discreet as possible, plastic-covered wire is the answer. This can hardly be seen on a brick wall, but of course it is only on this type of wall on which it can be used, as wall nails are necessary to hold the wire. It should be stretched in a pattern of six-inch to nine-inch squares on the wall, using wall nails to hold it firmly at the top and bottom and the sides. The wire must be kept about an inch from the wall so that the plant can weave its way through and spread over the wall. As the actual plant does not come into contact with the wall itself, no damage will be done, and if it is necessary at any time in the future to have repairs done, the plant can be pruned back, and the wire removed and replaced with new, after which the plant will grow up again quite happily. On walls where wiring is not possible, trellis work will have to be used.

Posts and pillars are effective means of supporting clematis, and the general effect of a pillar of colour in the garden is enchanting. Here the wire comes in useful again as our plant is incapable of climbing a foot-square pillar by itself. If the pillar is of brick, use wall nails both top and bottom, stretching the wire in between, then at intervals around the pillar, to give the plant something to cling to. A good idea where nails and wire are impracticable is to wrap a strip of wire netting round the pole, supporting it with a nail here and there. Always plant on the north side of a post or pillar, thus giving the roots that all-important shade.

In a wind-swept garden, post and pillars are not the best method, as the plant gets blown round to one side and the flowers are often bruised. The answer to this problem is to grow them on the ground. Trained over wire netting or pea-sticks pegged to the ground, they look most effective when seen from above. They can be kept low down from the worst of the wind, and should be pruned hard every winter to keep them clean and tidy. The Jackmanii types are the best for this purpose, as they flower for about three months and so provide a more or less permanent bedding plant. During the early part of the year, small bulbs could be used to fill the beds—the clematis will help to hide the dying bulb leaves so that during the rest of the summer and autumn we shall have a carpet of clematis, a new and exciting experience.

TRAINING

Training these bedding varieties calls for a little extra care, as the Jackmanii types will not flower on the lower parts of the stems ; so we must contrive to train the shoots round and over the spots likely to be bare of flower, that the surface of the bed may be evenly covered. When they have become well established, one can put a few higher stakes in the bed so that a pillar effect is obtained, rising from the bed of clematis.

FOUR : PRUNING

PRUNING often seems one of the greatest mysteries and stumbling-blocks in the growing of clematis, but it is really quite simple. All you have to do is find out when your plant blooms normally ; then if it is an early bloomer do not prune, but if it flowers late—that is, from July onwards—then prune hard every year, preferably in February, though it can be done equally well in the late autumn.

The great puzzle, of course, is to know when the normal flowering time is. Some varieties bloom from May to October, so how are you to determine when those plants should be pruned ? The answer is that if your clematis blooms profusely before June, then it belongs to the non-pruning section, even if it does carry on right through the summer till the autumn frosts. These are usually the Lanuginosa varieties, which flower just as freely on the young wood as on the old.

If they bloom profusely only from the end of June onwards, these are the varieties that bloom on the young wood, the Jack-manii and Viticella varieties, and they should be cut back hard every year. If left unpruned they will start growth from just below last year's flowering spot, and one is left with the bare stems at the bottom of the plant.

The only way to find out whether your plant is in the Patens, Lanuginosa or Jackmanii group is to leave it unpruned for a year ; then if it blooms freely in May and June with very large flowers, it belongs to the Patens group and should not be pruned. If it blooms during June or July on the old wood, and again in August or September on the young wood, it belongs to the

14

Lanuginosa group and need not be pruned. If it blooms from late June onwards on the young wood, producing masses of flowers non-stop until September or October, then it belongs to the Jackmanii or Viticella groups and must be pruned hard every February.

The earliest clematis to flower are the species, and they only have one flowering period, spring and early summer. These bloom on last year's wood, the flowers being produced directly from this old wood, so we must not prune after the first year. Into this category fall *C. alpina*, *C. armandii*, *C. calycina*, *C. chrysocoma*, *C. macropetala*, *C. montana*, *C. spooneri*, and *C. vedrariensis*. All these need plenty of room for expansion except *C. alpina* and *C. macropetala* and their varieties, which are ideal for small gardens. If they ever get out of hand and need trimming, the best time for pruning is directly *after* they have flowered. They can be cut back quite hard usually in June, leaving them with all the summer in which to recuperate and make plenty of wood for next year's flowering period. But in the main, leave them alone, let them ramble at will, and every spring they will be a joy to behold.

The next group to flower will be the Patens group. These are the plants that produce those enormous plate-like blooms, eight inches across, in May and June. They send out short side shoots from last year's wood, and it is on these that the magnificent flowers appear. No pruning is needed once the first-year build-up has been accomplished, but the plant must be trained properly to avoid a tangle of shoots that will become unmanageable in a year or two. If this should happen the plant can be pruned hard immediately after flowering so that strong young shoots are encouraged to develop during the summer and ripen into next year's flowering wood. In this section it is a good plan to look round the plant in March or April and trim back any dead ends to the shoots. Cut out any weak wood and generally tidy up the plant, tying it to its supports where necessary in order to give the flowering wood the best possible chance to display those eight-inch blooms that excite such admiration in early summer.

The Patens group include such well-known and well-loved varieties as blue ' Lasurstern ', purple ' The President ', violet ' Édouard Desfossé ', white ' Miss Bateman ', and the striped varieties ' Barbara Jackman ', ' Bee's Jubilee ', ' Bracebridge Star ', ' Lincoln Star ' and ' Nelly Moser '. A second period of flower is often obtained on the young wood in September in this section ; smaller flowers, not nearly so many, but very welcome all the same.

Flowering at the same time and needing the same treatment are the doubles, the Florida group. Double clematis are not everyone's choice, but there are one or two good ones—pale-mauve ' Belle of Woking ', mauve ' Countess of Lovelace ', white ' Duchess of Edinburgh ' and pink ' Proteus ' are four well-known varieties. One of the best is deep-violet-blue ' Vyvyan Pennell ', a striking variety. These only produce their double flowers on the old wood in the early summer ; single or semi-double flowers are often produced on the young wood in the late summer.

We now come to the group that causes all the bother, Lanuginosa. Varieties of this large-flowering section bloom from June to October, and pruning is often a puzzle here. They can be treated both ways : they can be left alone, or they can be pruned hard every February, thus adding to the confusion. The former method is the best, as we get the glorious and very large blooms on the old wood, followed, in many sorts, by a generous outburst of flower at different periods during the summer on the young wood. Thinning out in the spring is probably the best solution here, tying in the strong shoots and cutting out the weak ones. If the plant gets into too much of a tangle, cut it down quite ruthlessly in February and strong young shoots will develop from the base, bearing masses of medium-sized flowers in the late summer, with the promise of a glorious display of huge exotic blooms early the following year. Once you have a well-established plant of a Lanuginosa, with several shoots forming from the base, try relay pruning. That is, cut down half the plant in February, leaving half still on the wall. The part that is left will give you the fine early flowers, and the half you have cut down will shoot up during the early summer. You will get masses of smaller flowers on this new wood from July onwards. The following year, cut down the opposite sections, so that every two years the whole plant is cut down. This will probably cause a bit of trouble with training during the summer, but if the cut-down section can be trained on either side the first year, up the centre the second, one can keep out of trouble and have a good show all the summer. Some of the well-known varieties in this section are the blue ' Beauty of Worcester ' and ' Lady Northcliffe ', white ' Henryi ' and ' Madame le Coultre ', pale-mauve ' Blue Gem ' and ' W. E. Gladstone ', and lavender-mauve ' Mrs Cholmondeley ' and ' William Kennett '.

The next two groups to flower can be treated as one ; they are the Jackmanii and Viticella groups. The pruning and flowering period of these two are both the same. These varieties bear masses of medium-sized flowers throughout the summer right to the frosts of the late autumn, and as they bloom on the young wood the pruning treatment is simple. Prune hard every year— February is the best time, as this gives the plant time to ripen off thoroughly during the winter. They can, however, be cut back in the late autumn quite safely. The object of this ruthless pruning is to encourage the plant to develop strong young shoots to bear myriads of flowers during the summer. It is often feared that cutting back to a foot, or even less, is too drastic and that the plant will never recover in time, but watch those shoots grow ! When the days are warm in May and there is a good growing atmosphere, you can almost see them leaping up the wall. I have measured the rate of growth on humid days, and six inches in twenty-four hours is quite normal, so it does not take long to reclothe the wall or trellis, especially if we have been generous with manure and fertilisers in autumn and spring. Here again, relay pruning can be used to effect, by cutting down half a well-established plant in February and then a month later cutting the other half down. The first half will bloom normally from June to September, and the other half will bloom from July to October, thus prolonging the blooming season by a month at least. Varieties in this section include the famous purple ' Jackmanii ' and ' Gipsy Queen ', pink ' Comtesse de Bouchard ' and ' Hagley Hybrid ', white ' Huldine ', sky-blue ' Perle d'Azur ', and red ' Madame Édouard André ', ' Ernest Markham ' and ' Ville de Lyon '.

The late small-flowered species also come into this category of hard pruning, as they flower on the young wood late in the summer and throughout the autumn. So to get the best results, prune hard in February. These include all the varied coloured C. viticella, yellow C. tangutica and white C. flammula. But most people like to allow all the species to ramble at will, when they cover up to thirty or forty feet with ease, and are very graceful and useful plants, so that pruning of these varieties is not essential.

To put pruning in a nutshell :

Prune hard all late-flowering varieties, but those that bloom early, leave alone.

FIVE : DISEASES

Clematis do not suffer from many pests and diseases ; there is only one disease that causes any real trouble, and this is Clematis Wilt. This disease has been described as a ' killer ', the ' dreaded wilt ', or ' die-back ', and has been the cause of many young plants suddenly collapsing and dying for no apparent reason. The symptoms of wilt are a drooping of the growing tip ; the leaves and the buds will hang down as though the plant had been cut through with a knife. No-one knows the cause and, so far, no-one knows the cure—if there is a cure. The only thing we can do is to prevent its happening.

I am sure that if the instructions in Chapter Two are well and truly carried out, and the plant is kept low and not allowed to charge madly up the wall, outgrowing its strength, then all will be well. Quite a large part of these early failures are due to the plants' being neglected during their first year, and they are all classed as wilt victims. Kinking of the stems is often a major cause of many deaths, and even the hoe sometimes severs the stem with disastrous results. The wind also causes a number of failures that are attributed to wilt, but if the plant is well staked and tied to its support to prevent kinking and wind damage, then all will be safe if a sudden gale tears through the garden, or the enthusiastic hoer knocks against the plant. Cats and dogs can be another source of trouble for clematis, but a wirenetting cylinder round the base at the stem will keep them safe.

Another theory with regard to wilt suggests that the sudden hot spells in the summer, after a period of several dull days, is responsible for this collapse. I have seen this happening, myself. On a pergola planted with over thirty different varieties, I noticed on one very warm and humid day in the midst of a cool wet summer, that three young plants were drooping badly. Immediate action was taken, the plants cut right down to the base and kept well watered. Within a month they had started shooting again and the plants were saved. The respiratory system of the plants seems to be unable to cope with these abrupt changes in the weather and a light spraying of clear water night and morning will help the plant to adjust itself, but I am sure that the early and continuous pruning during the first year is the only answer.

Cheshunt Compound is another preventive measure ; this preparation is used to water seedlings, preventing damping-off and fungus, and as our dreaded Clematis Wilt is a fungus, this also helps in warding off an attack of the disease. Soak the ground around the plant in the spring, and at intervals during the growing season (about once a month) spray the plant completely. One could also use this compound during those sudden hot spells, for it does no harm to the plant and acts as a tonic. This need only be used during the first two seasons, as by the time your plant is well established it will be able to take care of itself. Jeypeat is another excellent preparation for warding off attacks of wilt.

If in spite of everything your plant suddenly collapses, then the only thing to do is to cut it right down, as low as possible and to just above a pair of buds. Just to water and spray the plant is useless, and prompt action with the knife is the only remedy left. The plant will take a few weeks to recover, but if it is cut down soon enough it will shoot up again and lose none of its vigour. The disease is a fungus and attacks one of the nodes on the stem, which it completely circles, cutting off all the sap to the growth above. If we find this spot and cut through it with a knife, we will see that the entire joint is brown and dead. Below this spot there is life, so if we cut down underneath to a pair of buds where the stem is green and fresh, we shall save the plant. To delay is fatal, as the fungus will penetrate downwards, killing the root and thus the whole plant. It is probably better to burn the diseased stems, although there is no danger of the attack spreading, for the strange thing about the wilt is that a plant is often attacked in the middle of several other varieties which come to no harm. It is also quite safe to plant in the same spot again, but a soaking of Cheshunt Compound before replanting is a wise move.

Mildew is another cause of trouble with some varieties of clematis, mainly the Jackmanii varieties, especially the red ones. This disfigures the plants rather than does them any harm, but the powdery deposits on leaf and flower are annoying, just when a blaze of colour is about to unfold. Our cold and wet climate is responsible for this minor trouble, and when we get a miserable summer, mildew is a great nuisance. Prevention here is again the best method, and there are several inexpensive remedies for mildew on the market ; but spraying with compound or dusting with green sulphur before the attack really takes hold is advisable, as once the powdery white mildew gets a firm hold it is very difficult to remove.

Earwigs are also a source of annoyance in the summer. These insects seem to delight in biting small holes in the flowers and leaves, disfiguring the whole plant. When a large number of them are present, whole flowers are gradually eaten away. Pyrethrum powder or D.D.T. dusted on the leaves late in the evening will repel these pests, or if one finds their hiding-place, a thorough spray of Sybol will destroy them. Earwigs usually enjoy their feast at night, hiding during the day under stones, bricks, in crevices and under bark in rustic work. If they can be exterminated here, the blooms of our plants will continue fresh and beautiful for their natural span of several weeks.

These are the three main clematis enemies. Slugs will sometimes do damage to the buds and young shoots, but they can be controlled quite easily with slug-bait, while ashes placed round the plant will deter these slimy pests—as will hunting them at night with the aid of a torch. So if our plants have been started off correctly, there is little to worry us, and the controlling of these few pests and diseases will not be very time-wasting or expensive.

Clematis, then, are practically free from disease. There is no need for the annual spray with fungicides or insecticides, often necessary with many other plants in the garden. Even the usual summer pests of green- and black-fly seldom infect a plant, so that, apart from the three afflictions named, our Virgin's Bower is disease- and trouble-free. Once it has grown into a strong healthy plant there will be little to worry about and we shall be able to look forward to many years of beauty and colour without pests or disease.

SIX : SPECIES

A WORLD of beauty exists in the small-flowering species or wild varieties of clematis. They garland the temperate regions of the earth with their myriads of blossoms in every shape and form. From the dainty bell-shaped *C. alpina* and *C. macropetala* to the star-like *C. montana*, pitcher-shaped *C. texensis*, lantern-shaped *C. tangutica* and saucer-shaped *C. viticella*. From the tiny *C. flammula*, barely a quarter of an inch across, to the enormous eight-inch *C. lanuginosa*, the largest of the species. Many of them have a delightful scent : *C. afoliata* gives us the scent of the daphne, *C. coerulea odorata* the aroma of a hawthorn hedge in May, *C. flammula* reminds us of vanilla and *C. rehderiana* of the cowslips in spring. *C. armandii*, *C. davidiana*, *C. jouiniana*, *C. montana* 'Alexander' and 'Elizabeth', *C. paniculata* and *C. vedrariensis rosea* all help to fill our gardens at various times of the year with their gentle perfume.

In addition to their radiant beauty and delicate fragrance, several of the species produce masses of feathery seed heads in the autumn. *C. alpina* and *C. macropetala* produce handsome 'whirligigs' during the summer, *C. flammula* gives us a cloud of silver grey in the autumn and *C. tangutica* sprouts thousands of handsome silky seed heads from July onwards.

Foliage in the species is also diverse in form. The small fern-like glossy green leaves of *C. calycina* are evergreen, as are the handsome three-lobed leaves of *C. armandii*. Most other varieties are deciduous and vary in size from the large coarse trifoliate leaves of *C. davidiana* to the small entire leaves of *C. flammula*.

Species will grow anywhere. They are remarkably trouble-free, and none of them suffers from Clematis Wilt, which only attacks their more exotic hybrid relations. Like the hybrids, they appreciate a cool moist root run and a mulching of manure every autumn. They are lime-loving plants and do exceptionally well on chalky soils. Several varieties are excellent for growing on cold north walls and in complete shade. These include well-known favourites, as C. *alpina*, C. *macropetala*, C. *montana*, C. *spooneri*, C. *vedrariensis* and their many varieties. They are also extremely useful for covering dead or uninteresting trees and shrubs, also sheds, garages and unsightly buildings. They are, of course, equally at home on the south wall in the full sun, but as there are so many good late-flowering varieties that must have a sunny spot, it seems a pity to waste them in such a position. The late-flowering varieties include the well-known C. *tangutica*, C. *flammula* and C. *viticella* and all their varieties, flowering from July to October. These are the only ones that need pruning, if at all, for when growing through trees and shrubs there is no need to cut them back—just let them ramble at will.

Although most of the species have small flowers, what they lack in size they make up for in numbers. Literally thousands of flowers appear during the season on great ropes of branches, festooning everything with their glory.

The true species will reproduce itself true from seed, but many of the varieties listed under species are really hybrids and do not come true from seed. This explains why there are so many different forms of C. *montana rubens*, some a good pink, but many of them a wishy-washy colour. Striking from cuttings is the only means of keeping good varieties true to form.

There are hundreds of species, from America, Europe, China— the home of so many gems of the garden—and even as far south as New Zealand. The following list contains the best of them. All are free-flowering, handsome and hardy in the British Isles. The only variety a little on the tender side is *C. armandii*, which requires a south wall when grown inland, though on the coast it is perfectly hardy.

C. AFOLIATA The rush-stemmed clematis. A curious plant from New Zealand which grows into a thick mass of green rush-like growths up to eight feet, and these become yellow in the winter. In the spring these growths are covered with tiny tubular pale-yellow flowers which have a very attractive scent like that of the daphne. As this variety blooms on the old wood only, it needs no pruning ; but if it gets too bushy, then the best time to prune it is directly after it has flowered.

C. ALPINA The ' Alpine Virgin's Bower ' has its natural habitat in the mountains of central and southern Europe, and is an ideal variety for growing over rock faces in the rock garden. Very early, *C. alpina* shows its first blooms in April and continues to delight us throughout the month of May. The flowers are single, four-sepalled, about two inches long, hang downwards and are of an exquisite shade of satiny blue. The stems are shaded with red in the early part of the year, turning to a normal brown as the season develops, and the bright-green three-lobed cut leaves are an attractive foil to the mountain blue of the flower. This variety is one of the Atragenes, a family closely allied to the clematis and now listed under them. The difference is that the Atragenes have a form of petal, while the clematis has only sepals and no petals of any sort. There are several varieties of *C. alpina* : a pale-lavender-blue variety called ' Columbine ', a wine-red variety called ' Ruby ' and a double white one named ' White Moth ', all most useful plants. None of these varieties is tall and the general height is six to eight feet with about the same dimensions in width.

C. ARMANDII The best of the evergreens. The leaves of this variety are large and often eight inches long, three-lobed and glossy green. Even when not in flower, the plant is a most handsome specimen for a south or west wall, and although slightly tender, this Chinese variety *can* be grown on a sunny and sheltered wall where it will develop quickly into a large and vigorous plant, growing to a height of thirty feet and more, and covering several feet in width. When the plant has reached the maximum height available, great rope-like branches will grow and hang down for several feet, and these during March and April are covered with masses of small waxy-white flowers one inch to two inches in diameter, with a vanilla perfume. Clusters of these flowers develop at each leaf axil and present quite a charming picture in the spring. There are two other varieties, ' Apple Blossom ', a pale pink, and ' Snowdrift ', a larger white. Pruning is sometimes a problem, as when the plant is several years old, layer upon layer of shoots will descend and those underneath become sear and brown. To keep the plant green and attractive, thin out the shoots after flowering, cutting back the flowering wood and allowing the young strong shoots to develop during the summer.

C. *CALYCINA* is the earliest of all to flower, and during any of the mild spells from January to March we may get a profusion of dainty little bell-shaped flowers. These are pale yellow, and the inside of the flower is freckled with red. The great advantage of C. *calycina* is that it is evergreen. The leaves are small and fern-like, which gives it the popular name ' The Fern-leaved Clematis '. It is a fast-growing plant and makes in time quite a thick mass of stems, all covered with charming little lemon bells. C. *calycina* has another name as well, C. *balearica*, to remind us of its place of origin, the Balearic Islands in the Mediterranean, where this variety grows wild. In time this winter-flowering clematis will attain a height of twenty to thirty feet, and will grow quite happily along a low wall or fence and form a dense bush. This valuable evergreen never needs any pruning, but it can be cut back hard after flowering if it is necessary to keep it in bounds. Young plants do not always produce flowers freely, and it takes two or three years for the plant to become established and start blooming profusely.

C. CIRRHOSA This is another evergreen, although not such a good colour as C. calycina. It gives plenty of bloom on the young plants, is cream in colour and flowers freely during the early months of the year. The popular name is the ' Evergreen Virgin's Bower '. The leaves are broader than those of C. calycina and more glossy green. Both will grow quite well in shade and even on a north wall, but to get the best display of flower they should be on a warm south wall, or scrambling through shrubs in a sheltered spot in the garden.

C. CAMPANIFLORA The ' Harebell Virgin's Bower ' is very aptly named, as the small bell-shaped flowers hang from the stems, looking like miniature harebells. A native of Portugal, it is a vigorous climber and flowers from July to September. The leaves are cut into a number of leaflets. As it flowers on the young wood, it should be pruned hard in February ; but if growing through trees and shrubs, it can be left to ramble at will, making a very attractive and dainty contribution to its host.

C. CHRYSOCOMA The ' Hairy Clematis '. The reason for the peculiar popular name is that the young shoots are covered with minute golden-brown hairs. This splendid variety was introduced from China in 1910, when it was found growing wild on the mountain slopes of Yunnan. Why it should still be very little known is a bit of a mystery, as this is by far the best of the Montana group. It is a very robust grower, and its rope-like branches are covered in May and June with masses of soft-pink flowers produced in clusters, on quite long stems too. The added advantage of this variety is its extended season of flower ;

normally the Montana group flowers only during May and June, but this one flowers during the rest of the summer on the young wood—not all the time, of course, but in bursts of quite a number of flowers at odd times from July to September. These later flowers are a pale colour, being almost white, but their appearance is always a delight and adds a touch of springtime to the garden. *C. chrysocoma* does not need pruning, but its vigour is such that a little thinning-out is necessary at times or the beauty of the plant will be lost. After the flowering season is the best time to thin out the weak wood and cut off any wood that has flowered. New shoots will quickly develop and should be allowed to ramble at will through trees, shrubs or over walls and pergolas. A height of thirty feet will easily be covered in a season with this variety, and it will cover a similar area if trained horizontally.

C. COERULEA ODORATA A semi-herbaceous variety with small four-sepalled reddish-purple flowers produced in abundance from early July until late autumn. An unusual feature of the flowers is the prominent white staminal filaments, which stand out like a small thistle. The scent of this variety is of hawthorn blossom, and it is quite strong. The usual height is about six feet, and the stems have to be tied to some support. The leaves vary from single ovate to three-lobed, moderate in size. This variety should be pruned hard every February.

C. DAVIDIANA This was introduced by M. l'Abbé David in 1864 from the French garden at Pe-che-le in northern China. It is a herbaceous variety which makes a bushy plant about two to three feet high, with large ternate leaves and the bright-blue tubular flowers, sweet-scented, resembling hyacinths, produced in clusters all down the stem. The flowering period is September to October. Hard pruning is needed each spring, removing last season's dead shoots.

C. ERIOSTEMON   The first hybrid to be raised in this country in 1836 by Mr Henderson, and originally called *C. hendersonii*. It is a cross between *C. viticella* and *C. integrifolia* ; the leaves are similar to the simple leaves of the latter variety, whilst the flowers, which are produced very abundantly from July to October, are similar to those of *C. viticella*, though slightly larger, nodding, four-sepalled and purple-blue. The plant grows to a height of twelve feet, and should be pruned hard in February. Usually, however, this variety dies down to the ground in the winter.

C. FARGESII   This variety was introduced from China by E. H. Wilson in 1911. It produces masses of six-sepalled white flowers similar to the flowers of the blackberry, from June until the autumn. The foliage is downy and the young shoots are tinged with purple. It is a vigorous and rapid grower, blooming on the young wood, and so is best pruned hard in the spring.

C. FLAMMULA   The ' Fragrant Virgin's Bower '—and rightly named, too ! In the autumn this delightful plant is a billowy mass of tiny white flowers, when many thousands of the little blooms are out at the same time, transforming the plant into a living snow-storm, exquisitely scented. When the air is moist, as it often is in September and October, the fragrance of vanilla from these tiny flowers drifts over the whole garden. The leaves are dark green and almost evergreen, staying on the plant long after the deciduous clematis have shed their leaves, and often throughout the season in a mild winter. Pruning with this variety can also be hard, as it is with all late-flowering varieties that bloom on the young wood, but if grown in trees or shrubs it can be left unpruned. The plant will make up to fifteen feet of growth in a year, and almost as much in width, so it is ideal for covering bushes and small trees. The masses of feathery seed heads that follow the flower are also most decorative and useful in floral decoration. *C. flammula rubra marginata* is a cross between *C. flammula* and *C. viticella*, with masses of tiny flowers with a rosy-purple band round each small sepal, paler in the centre, with a close tuft of green stamens. This variety is also sweetly scented.

C. FLORIDA BICOLOR A native of Japan, this rare and beautiful clematis blooms from July to September. The flowers are six-sepalled, creamy white, with a densely packed mass of petaloid stamens of a rich purple in the centre, thus providing an attractive contrast in colour. The flowers are fairly large for the species, about four inches in diameter. The buds are produced on long stems, and when the flowers first open they are greenish white. Even after the sepals have dropped, the purple-rosette centre remains attractive for some time. The growth is slender, and the foliage is light and feathery, making a very attractive but sometimes difficult plant to establish. A warm corner is advised, with some protection during the winter, until the plant is strong enough to withstand the damp and fog of an English winter.

C. INTEGRIFOLIA A very old variety, which has probably been in our gardens for three or four hundred years. A low-growing herbaceous variety, *C. integrifolia* has erect stems, entire ovate-lanceole leaves, and produces single nodding purple-blue flowers from July onwards. *C. integrifolia durandii* is a cross between *C. integrifolia* and *C. lanuginosa* and grows to a height of six feet with entire leaves. The flowers, five inches across, open much wider than those of the type, are four-sepalled, deeply veined, and of a vivid deep blue. The plant flowers from June to October. It needs support and should be pruned hard every February. Another form is *C. integrifolia hendersonii*, a variety of medium growth with lavender-blue nodding flowers. July and

August is the flowering period. This, too, needs tying to a support.

C. JOUINIANA The leaves of this late-flowering variety are large, and during the autumn the plant is covered with thousands of small hyacinth-like flowers, pale blue, giving the appearance of a pale-blue haze over the whole plant. During the season long growths will appear, making it an ideal plant for covering tree stumps or small buildings. This is not a climbing variety, however, and the stems must be attached to their supports. It can be very useful as ground cover and can be pruned hard in the early spring. Two varieties which do not grow so high, making bushes of about four feet, are ' Campanile ' and ' Cote d'Azur '. The former sends up strong shoots which are covered in the late summer with pale-blue sweetly scented flowers, produced in generous clusters at every leaf axil. The latter variety is of taller growth and looser habit, but with deeper blue flowers. Both varieties should be cut down to the ground in February.

C. LANUGINOSA The largest-flowered of all the species, fully eight inches across. This lovely variety comes to us from China, and was collected by Robert Fortune. The buds and leaves are woolly, which gives it the name of the ' Woolly-leaved Clematis ', and it flowers from June to September. The colour is pale lavender and it is star-shaped. The plant rarely attains a greater height than eight feet, and the leaves are simple and ternate. This variety is one of the parents of many of the well-known large-flowering hybrids of the modern garden.

A white variety of the *C. lanuginosa*, called *C. lanuginosa candida*, produces large flowers of a grey-white when opening but developing to a pure white ; the large number of sepals, up to twelve sometimes, gives it the appearance of a semi-double flower. The buds are woolly as in the type.

C. MACROPETALA is one of the loveliest of all the species,

31

and in the spring its lavender-blue nodding flowers are a delight to see. They are produced freely during May and June, and cover the plant from top to bottom. Normally C. *macropetala* is not a tall-growing plant, its average height being usually about eight to ten feet, but I have seen specimens over twenty feet high, and looking up to the semi-double flowers is a rare experience. A native of China, this variety is called the ' Downy Clematis ', as the flowers are covered with down. They are semi-double, with inch-long sepals that hang down looking for all the world like fairy ballet skirts. The foliage is similar to that of C. *alpina*, and we find that C. *macropetala* is another of the Atragene section. This variety has only been in our gardens since 1912—and very few gardens at that. Now, however, the general public is beginning to discover this delightful and very beautiful clematis. There is a deep-blue variety called ' Lagoon ', a mid-blue named ' Maidwell Hall ' and a lovely mauve-pink variety called C. *macropetala Markhamii,* one of the many fine clematis raised by that famous grower of clematis, Ernest Markham. This variety is ideal for the north wall, although of course it will thrive and grow anywhere in the garden. Pruning is hardly necessary, as C. *macropetala* flowers on year-old wood and, never growing rampant, does not have to be restricted in any way. Any tidying up and removal of old wood could be done in the winter, but if actual pruning is ever necessary, then directly after flowering is the best time.

C. *MONTANA* The ' Mountain Clematis ', ' Great Indian Clematis ', C. *anemoneflora* or C. *odorata*—call it what you will— is one of the most valuable and ornamental climbers we possess. Introduced from the Himalayas in 1831, this variety flowers in May and June, when the thirty- to forty-foot-long stems are wreathed in pure white anemone-like flowers. A vigorous climber, it must have room to develop, and if left alone will wreathe everything in its reach with great beauty in the spring and early summer. When originally introduced into our gardens, *C. montana* had a sweet scent, which explains the fourth name given to it, but during the course of time, owing to stock being raised from seed, the scent has disappeared and the size of the flower has decreased. A variety which has recently been introduced from India may be synonymous with the original *C. montana* of 1840. The flowers are very large, each sepal being over one inch in length, giving a three-inch flower, and the scent is delicious. This was brought to England by Col. R. D. Alexander, and so is called *C. montana* ' Alexander '. The leaves, which are ternate, are also much larger than those of our *C. montana* of today. Propagated from cuttings and layers only, this fine variety should retain its size and scent.

A good-scented pink variety is *C. montana* ' Elizabeth '. The four-sepalled flowers are over two inches in diameter, a pale pink, and delightfully scented. The leaves, ternate, have a bronzy hue and like all the Montana group it flowers during May and June.

A particularly good form of pink is *C. montana rubens*, the ' Rosy Virgin's Bower '. The flowers are about two inches in diameter, and consist of four rounded sepals with a tuft of straw-coloured stamens in the centre, and they are produced in thousands. The branches have several flowers at every leaf axil, so that we have floral ropes covering the plant. The foliage has a bronzy hue, adding to the general attraction of the deep-pink flowers. The variety is not quite so vigorous as the type, but is just as hardy.

C. montana Wilsonii is a useful addition to this family, as it flowers later, during June and July, and the strongly scented creamy-white flowers are curious, each sepal being twisted. Pruning of all these varieties is hardly ever necessary, but sometimes they do get out of hand, and then some remedy has to be found. The best time to cut back the plant is directly after it has flowered, which will be some time in June. It can be cut back quite hard, as new shoots will soon form again on the old wood, and before the end of the summer will have grown twenty feet or more. They can even be trimmed off whilst in full growth if necessary, as clematis do not seem to mind being cut back at any time of the year. Normally, however, a thinning-out during the winter will be all that is necessary and, providing we have given the plant plenty of room to expand, it will wreathe everything with its beauty in the late spring and early summer. All in the Montana group are ideal plants for cold north walls and for clothing dead and uninteresting trees.

C. *NEPALENSIS* This peculiar variety, as its name suggests, comes from Nepal. An evergreen, it blooms freely in the winter from January to March with curious creamy-yellow flowers, with a tuft of reddish-purple stamens, produced in clusters from the leaf axils. During the summer this variety often looks dead, but with the arrival of cooler weather fresh green shoots will appear. It will grow to a height of twenty feet or more, and little pruning is necessary.

C. *ORIENTALIS* Also called C. *graveolens*, a rare and lovely variety. The flowers are orange or deep yellow, and hang down, and each of the four thick sepals opens wide. The leaves are grey-green, finely cut, giving the plant a graceful and delicate appearance. The flowers appear in late summer and autumn, and their thick sepals give it the popular name of the ' Orange Peel Clematis '. Feathery seed heads quickly follow the flowers, adding to the beauty of the plant. Growths are slender, and the plant will attain a height of fifteen feet. Moderate pruning should be the rule with this elegant climber.

C. *PANICULATA* Semi-evergreen variety, similar to C. *flam-*

mula, producing masses of small fragrant white flowers in late summer and autumn. The leaves and flowers are larger than those of *C. flammula*. This variety has become very popular in the U.S.A., where it is known as the ' Sweet Autumn Clematis '.

C. RECTA The white Herbaceous Virgins Bower. This variety has been in our gardens for hundreds of years and is an ideal variety for cut flowers with its long erect stems of two to three feet pannicles of small white, fragrant flowers produced freely during the summer. Hard pruning down to the ground during the winter is necessary with this herbacous variety.

C. REHDERIANA A most unusual variety. Called the ' Nodding Virgin's Bower ', this clematis actually smells of cowslips— and quite strongly too. This, mark you, in the autumn ! So when growing *C. rehderiana*, or *C. nutans* as it is also called, we get a breath of spring in the fall of the year. It makes a large plant and will grow to a height of twenty feet. The leaves are a little coarse and not very interesting, but from the axil of each leaf a loose cluster of little flowers is produced in September and October. They are small and greenish-yellow in colour, each little bell-like nodding flower turning up quaintly at the ends of the sepals, rather like the turn-up on a trouser leg. The stems on which they are produced are several inches long, and when the whole plant is in bloom it is quite charming. Pruning should be done in February and should be severe, as the plant will grow rapidly during the summer and flower on the young wood.

C. SERRATIFOLIA A native of Korea, the ' Cut-leaved Clematis ' is a climber of slender growth. The pale-yellow flowers are nodding, with purple stamens, and produced during the late summer and early autumn. In the autumn the plant is covered with attractive silky seed heads. Hard pruning should be the rule in February, and the plant will grow to a height of twelve feet during the summer.

C. SPOONERI This is, I think, a better variety than the more common *C. montana* ; the flowers are much larger, more beautiful, and they are produced with almost as great a profusion in May and June. Belonging to the Montana section, *C. spooneri* is a very fine variety indeed, and ideal for the north wall. The flowers are four-sepalled, of a pure white with a charming yellow centre. The leaves are quite distinct, being covered with small chestnut-coloured hairs, giving them a unique appearance. The growths are also different, the bronzy hue of the summer turning to almost black during the winter. Not quite so rampant as *C. montana*, it is the ideal plant for the smaller garden, and does not need any pruning beyond thinning out during the winter if necessary. If drastic pruning is needed, then treat it in the same way as *C. montana*. *C. spooneri rosea* is a good pink form with attractive ' winged ' sepals.

C. TANGUTICA This is a bright-yellow clematis, a colour that is quite unknown as yet in the large-flowering hybrid, though in the species we have several varieties, lemon and pale yellow, with *C. tangutica* far and away the best. It is a strong grower and will rapidly climb up to twenty feet in a season, and does best when it is pruned hard every February, as with the Jackmanii types, almost down to the ground. The multitude of flowers are produced on the young wood, so hard pruning will encourage the necessary growth. This variety is known as the ' Russian Virgin's Bower ', and is native to that part of the world. The flowers are lantern-shaped, about one to two inches in diameter, and have four sepals ; they hang in great profusion all over the plant. It begins flowering in midsummer and will continue right through without a break until the end of October. As soon as the first flowers fade, they quickly develop into charming silky heads, and by the end of August, and for the rest of the season, the plant is smothered in a billowy mass of silver-grey. Hundreds of flowers are opening all the time and hang in a golden mass on the plant, intermingling with the seed heads—a silky cloud with hundreds of yellow lanterns. This variety will grow practically anywhere, through trees, on walls, pergolas, etc., and I have even seen it flowering freely on a north wall ; but its favourite spot is on a south wall in the sun.

C. *TEXENSIS* The Texensis group comes from the state of Texas in America ; they are semi-herbaceous, and die down to the ground every winter. The true type is also known as C. *coccinea*, and is a bright fiery red, and shaped like a pitcher with turned-back points to the sepals, revealing the buff-pink lining. The flowers, which never open fully as those of other clematis do, are fleshy in texture, and remain on the plant for several weeks from June to the end of September. The form C. *texensis* ' Gravetye Beauty ', a handsome and rare variety, was raised at the famous Gravetye Manor in Sussex, the home of William Robinson (author of *The English Flower Garden*), with Ernest Markham, his head gardener. The flowers open wider than those of the type. The sepals are about two inches long, four in number, and are produced on long stems from July to October in quite good quantity and of a glorious bright red. The foliage is a glaucous green, making a very effective background to these graceful flowers. C. *texensis* ' Gravetye Beauty ' is not a tall grower, and for a small garden is an excellent variety, as it never attains much more than six feet. C. *texensis* ' Duchess of Albany ' is a good pink variety, having bell-shaped flowers with a deep-pink bar—a good late-summer- and autumn-flowering variety. Pruning is simple, as all that needs to be done is to remove the dead wood in February ; and as most plants die down to the ground in the winter, this simply means removing all top growth.

C. *VEDRARIENSIS ROSEA* A variety that belongs to the Montana section and flowers at the same time—May and June.

The four-sepalled flowers are a pale pink, sweetly scented and produced in great profusion. *C. vedrariensis* ' Highdown ' is an improved variety. The blooms are large, about two and a half inches across, of a lovely delicate pink, the reverse being a deeper colour. These flowers are produced freely on long stems from very distinctive deep-green foliage which is much larger than that of the Montana types and very handsome. This variety needs no pruning and will eventually cover thirty or forty feet with ease. Both sorts are ideal for cold north walls and shady spots in the garden.

C. *VITALBA* The ' Old Man's Beard ' or ' Traveller's Joy ' of the English hedgerows. The only clematis native to this country, it is a vigorous climber covering up to thirty feet or more in a single season. The flowers, produced in August, are greenish-white, small and not very conspicuous. They are followed, however, by masses of billowy seed heads which cover hedges and even trees with a curtain of silver-grey foam during the autumn and early winter. An ideal variety to grow quickly over unsightly objects.

C. *VITICELLA* The ' Virgin's Bower '. The first clematis to be brought into this country, it came from Spain during the reign of the first Queen Elizabeth. The popular name of ' Virgin's Bower ' may have been given to the plant at the time as a tribute to the queen. The flowers are produced in great numbers during the late summer and early autumn. They are saucer-shaped and hang down, one or two inches in diameter, and as the plant is a vigorous climber, we have the great pleasure of looking *up* at these delightful little blooms. There are several varieties of C. *viticella* : the pure-white form known as *C. v. alba luxurians*, soft purple ' Abundance ', a good red variety called ' Kermesina ', the slaty-blue ' Little Nell ', and a fine form called ' Minuet ', which has larger flowers than the type, creamy-white in the centre with a band of purple round each sepal. These exquisite blooms are produced on very long stems throughout the summer. To complete the family we have the velvet-purple ' Royal Velour ', and the crimson *C. v. rubra*, an outstanding variety. To get the best results prune hard early every year.

SEVEN : THE BEST LARGE-FLOWERING HYBRIDS

SINCE 1860, when large-flowering hybrids first became all the rage, many hundreds of different varieties have been raised. Many have been discarded and superseded, and some wonderful Victorian names have disappeared—varieties such as Beauty of the Bower, Gloire de St Julien, Lady Stratford de Redcliffe, to name only three. Most of them were greyish-blue or off-white, and soon disappeared as increasing numbers of nurserymen and amateur gardeners improved on the old varieties, and better colours were introduced. Even now there are far too many varieties of a similar colour, and it is only on close examination that their differences can be determined.

The following lists contain the best of the hybrids, the best colours, the hardiest and strongest growing, and the most free-flowering varieties. They are divided into three groups of twelve in each group, so that the gardener may know the most reliable varieties to choose for different times of the year. Each variety is described later on in alphabetical order.

SPRING AND EARLY-SUMMER-FLOWERING VARIETIES THAT NEED NO PRUNING

Barbara Dibley	Lasurstern
Barbara Jackman	Lincoln Star
Bee's Jubilee	Miss Bateman
Duchess of Edinburgh	Nelly Moser
Édouard Desfossé	The President
Kathleen Dunford	Vyvyan Pennell

THE BEST LARGE-FLOWERING HYBRIDS

All these varieties belong to the Patens and Florida groups, which produce their flowers on short terminal growths from the old wood, and so there is no need for pruning once the plant is established. Good training is essential though.

EARLY-SUMMER-TO-AUTUMN-FLOWERING VARIETIES THAT NEED NO PRUNING

Beauty of Worcester	Lady Northcliffe
Elsa Spath	Madame le Coultre
Fairy Queen	Mrs Cholmondeley
Henryi	Prins Hendrik
King George V	W. E. Gladstone
Lady Caroline Neville	William Kennett

These varieties belong to the Lanuginosa group ; there are many varieties in this section, and they cover a wide range of colour and of flowering period. They should be left unpruned, as the largest blooms are produced on the year-old wood. The young wood also produces a mass of flower, so in this section we get some of the longest-flowering varieties in clematis. Here again a well trained plant must be the aim.

SUMMER-AND-AUTUMN-FLOWERING VARIETIES THAT SHOULD BE PRUNED HARD EVERY YEAR

Comtesse de Bouchard	Jackmanii
Ernest Markham	Lady Betty Balfour
Étoile Violette	Madame Édouard André
Gipsy Queen	Perle d'Azur
Hagley Hybrid	Victoria
Huldine	Ville de Lyon

These varieties belong to the Jackmanii and Viticella groups, and they do certainly need hard pruning every year. This should be done early in February, when the buds start to swell, down to the lowest pair of buds on each stem. One need not always stick to the rule, however, as there are cases where the purple Jackmanii has been left unpruned and it has covered an enormous area. The only snag is that the base of the plant will be left rather bare, as in the Jackmanii group the flower is only produced on the end of the new shoots and there is invariably a certain amount of growth before flowering wood is produced.

VARIETIES IN ALPHABETICAL ORDER

BARBARA DIBLEY Rich deep pansy-violet. A wonderful colour that almost defies description and which is quite new to clematis. When the large eight-inch-wide flowers first open, the colour is very deep indeed. After a few days this vivid colour fades a little, to reveal a broad deep bar down the centre of the sepals, which are six to eight in number. These are long and broad, making a fine full flower. The normal flowering time is May and June, but a really good second crop appears in August and September. These later flowers are not so large and not so deep in colour, but they are very handsome indeed. Barbara Dibley grows to a height of eight to ten feet, needs no pruning and will grow in any position. Especially good on a north wall, where the colour will not fade.

BARBARA JACKMAN A very fine variety. The colour base of the flower, which measures about six inches in diameter, is soft petunia, and down the centre of each sepal runs a wide bar of a striking violet-crimson colour. Its centre-piece is most attractive, with a mass of cream-coloured stamens, which contrast most effectively with the exotic colouring of the sepals. May and June is the flowering time. The sepals number five or six, and they are exquisitely formed, giving each flower an almost perfect shape. The bar will fade with age, and after the flower has been out for a fortnight it will almost disappear—but still leaving a flower of great beauty. Planted on a north or north-west wall, this variety will bring out its best colouring, and in this position the bar will not fade. Barbara Jackman makes a plant of about six to eight feet tall, and four to five feet wide. No pruning is necessary, after one has obtained a nice bushy plant during the first year, as this variety blooms on the old wood. In the late summer one is lucky enough, sometimes, to get a good show on the young wood. The flowers may not be so large as the early ones but the colour is just as good.

BEAUTY OF WORCESTER One of the finest blue clematis in cultivation, this variety is a good deep violet-blue. The sepals, eight in number, are of medium size but of a good width so that the flower, about six inches in diameter, has complete fullness. The prominent white stamens set the blue off to perfection, and a well-grown plant will bear two or three hundred blooms from June to October. The unique fact about this clematis is that it produces double and single flowers during the same season. The double flowers are produced on the old wood during June and July, and the lovely single flowers follow on the young wood right through the summer, and often well into the autumn. A fine and impressive variety for south and west aspects, which will eventually make a plant of eight to twelve feet in height and four to six feet in width.

BEE'S JUBILEE Another wonderful striped variety. Often described as an improved Nelly Moser, although the centre is less striking. The colour is, however, a great improvement, being a deep mauve-pink with a deep-crimson bar down the centre of each of the eights sepals. The flowers with rounded sepals are very large, often measuring over eight inches across, and they are borne in great profusion during May and June on the old wood, and again very freely in September and October on the young wood. As the colour is so much stronger, it can be planted safely on a south wall and will not bleach as Nelly Moser does. Bee's Jubilee will grow to a height of between ten and fifteen feet and four to six feet in width. It belongs to the Patens group, so there is no need to prune after the first year. All that is needed in the future is to trim back the dead ends in the early spring.

COMTESSE DE BOUCHARD One of the best pink clematis in cultivation, producing masses of flower from June to the end of September. The individual flowers are saucer-shaped and are a lovely shade of rose-pink. The flowers are about five to six inches across ; the rounded sepals, six in number, are wide and incurving, giving the flower a full appearance and the distinctive saucer-shape design. The stamens are yellow and not as bold as in the other groups, but the whole effect of the plant when in flower is of an unbroken mass of rich rose-pink blossom. It makes quite a bushy plant and is often as wide as it is high. Normally eight to twelve feet is its limit, but it will grow much higher in favoured positions. A good variety for any aspect.

DUCHESS OF EDINBURGH A double white clematis belonging to the Florida group. This old variety has been popular for almost a hundred years. The flowers are very double : there are about ten to twelve rows of sepals, giving the flower the appearance of a guelder rose or a dahlia. A circlet of leaves just below the flower heightens a curious appearance just before the buds open, half leaves, half sepals ; they are greenish-white and curiously twisted. Duchess of Edinburgh flowers during May and June, and it is only then that the completely double flowers are produced. Often one gets semi-double flowers in the late summer, but these are much less attractive. This variety, which has a slight scent, will grow to a height of eight to ten feet, and will grow on a south or west wall.

EDOUARD DESFOSSÉ This variety is reputed to be the largest flowering of all clematis, the huge deep violet-mauve flowers with a deeper bar on each sepal are produced from the old wood in May and it is the earliest of all the hybrids. The blooms are often eight to ten inches across, but are not very free in numbers. Edouard Desfossé prefers quality to quantity. Belonging to the Patens group little pruning is necessary. It will make a plant of twelve to fifteen feet in height and prefers a south or west aspect.

ELSA SPATH A really good deep-blue clematis which flowers from July to September, in medium size with pointed sepals and dark stamens. Elsa Spath belongs to the Lanuginosa family and needs little pruning after the first year, as it bears flowers on both the old and young wood. A little tidying up in the spring is all that is needed, and if the plant does get into a tangle it can always be cut down in February, as one would for the Jackmanii group, and it will flower freely on the young wood in August and September. It makes a medium-sized plant of about eight feet for a south or west aspect, and is ideal for the small garden.

ERNEST MARKHAM Named after one of the most famous names in clematis history. With William Robinson at Gravetye Manor in Sussex, Ernest Markham grew and raised many new varieties. The variety named after him is generally recognised as the best red clematis in existence. Late flowering, during September and October, makes this variety especially useful, but it must be on a sunny wall. The colour is a good rich petunia-red ; the flowers are of a medium size, and the sepals, six in number, are rounded. Pruning should be carried out every year in

February, cutting the plant down as hard as possible, but if left unpruned this variety will produce flowers on the old wood in May and June, though the best show of flowers is in September

ÉTOILE VIOLETTE   A good midsummer variety which produces thousands of four-sepalled flowers all July and August. It belongs to the Jackmanii group and is similar in colour to Jackmanii, though deeper, with bright-yellow stamens. Étoile Violette will ramp over fences and bushes, festooning the whole area with a mantle of purple. It is a vigorous grower, will make a plant of fifteen to twenty feet in one season, and is suitable for any aspect. Hard pruning every year is essential, as it flowers on the young wood only.

FAIRY QUEEN   Most of the striped clematis seem to belong to the Patens group, but this very lovely variety belongs to the Lanuginosa group, and flowers during the summer. The huge, often nine-inch-wide blooms are a delicate flesh-pink, and down the centre of each sepal there is a broad pale-pink bar. Each bloom is exquisitely formed and very beautiful. Fairy Queen, aptly named, needs little pruning. It flowers quite freely on both young and old wood, and will make a plant of up to twelve feet. A south or west aspect is best for this variety.

GIPSY QUEEN   A good late-flowering variety. The rich velvet-purple flowers are produced in masses from August until well into October. The colour is much deeper than that of Jackmanii, although the flowers are about the same size ; up to six sepals are produced on each flower, however. Requiring hard pruning, this variety will grow up to fifteen feet with ease. As it is a late variety, it must be planted on a south wall.

HAGLEY HYBRID   A beautiful shell-pink with attractive brown stamens. This lovely free-flowering variety blooms from June to late September, and the first flowers are really exquisite : large for a Jackmanii variety, they measure well over six inches in diameter, and the sepals, four to six in number and pointed, make a shapely flower. An ideal plant for the small garden, Hagley Hybrid can be planted in any position. Never growing much over six feet, it makes a nice bushy plant and should be pruned hard every February.

HENRYI This clematis, which also goes under the name of Bangholme Belle, is a glorious white. The enormous flowers, often over eight inches in diameter, are freely produced in June and July on the old wood. Smaller but equally lovely flowers appear on the young wood until October. The centre of the flowers is dark, the stamens being a deep brown. When first opening, the flowers often have a pale-green stripe down the centre of the sepals, but this soon disappears, leaving the pure-white magnificent blooms on their stiff sturdy stems to enchant us for weeks on end. If cut, they will last in water for well over a fortnight and make a most exotic table decoration. Henryi will make a bushy plant up to eighteen feet high, and is a good strong reliable variety for a south or west aspect.

HULDINE One of the few white varieties in the Jackmanii and Viticella groups. This very strong and vigorous variety bears masses of pearly-white flowers from July to October. The blooms are not large, about four to five inches across, but they are produced very freely and they are ideal for use as a cut flower. The backs of the sepals, which vary in number from four to six, have a pale-mauve bar, and when seen with the light shining through the semi-translucent flowers they have a quite unique beauty, distinct from that of all other clematis. A rapid and robust grower, Huldine will make up to twenty feet of growth annually, and needs hard pruning in February. Sometimes this variety makes so much growth that it forgets to flower, and if this happens the remedy is quite simple : just cut back the growing shoots. It does not matter where : simply pinching out the tips

47

will do, but more often than not these tips are way out of reach before we realise that we have no flowers, and in this case a pair of shears will do to cut all the top growth off. This should be done in midsummer, and within a few weeks new shoots will be bursting all over the place, but this time they will be flowering wood, and the dainty flowers of Huldine will delight us until the frosts come. A good variety for a sunny position.

JACKMANII The most famous of all clematis. This well-known and beloved clematis was raised in 1858 and first flowered in 1862 ; it was the variety that started the clematis craze of the nineteenth century. An established plant will attain a height of twenty feet in a season—that is, after being pruned down almost to the ground in February. The speed with which they climb is amazing, and on a good-growing day they can almost be seen climbing up the wall. The masses of purple flowers are produced freely from June until September. The individual flowers are five to six inches in diameter. The sepals are four to six in number, rounded in shape and rather open at the base, so that the flower is not so full as others in this section. The centre is composed of a small tuft of greenish stamens. Jackmanii superba has broader sepals than the ordinary Jackmanii, and is a deeper purple, but is rather inclined to mildew badly. Both varieties are ideal for any position in the garden, even cold north walls.

In a book on clematis published in 1877, there is an account of a Jackmanii planted in Scotland, which after the first year was deliberately left unpruned. As the shoots developed they were all tied in neatly, and the only pruning consisted of the removal of the flowering wood. The plant attained an area of fifteen feet square, was bearing twelve hundred blossoms at one time, and it was capable of doubling the area if space had been available.

KATHLEEN DUNFORD Raised from a chance seedling in the

early 1950s, this exciting new clematis is quite different from all other varieties. It is semi-double, but whereas all the other semi-double varieties have an outer circle of large sepals, with an inner circle of much smaller ones, Kathleen Dunford has two layers of sepals, both the same size ! The flowers are large with six to eight sepals, or rather twelve to sixteen, and the colour is a rich rose-purple with a deeper bar down the centre of each sepal. The stamens are golden brown and the leaves have a bronzy hue. Flowering time is May and June as this lovely variety belongs to the Patens group, but single flowers are produced on the young wood in August and September. The plant grows to a height of eight to ten feet and is an ideal variety for the small garden. No pruning is required.

KING GEORGE V This is another of the few striped varieties in the Lanuginosa group flowering in the summer, whereas nearly all the striped varieties flower in the spring. King George V is flesh-pink with a red bar down the centre of each pointed sepal, and needs a south or west wall. The flowers are of medium size, about five to six inches across, saucer-shaped and produced freely during July and August. This is a useful variety for the smal garden, as it is not too vigorous and makes a plant of about eight to ten feet. No pruning is necessary, but as it belongs to the Lanuginosa group it can be cut down if necessary in February and it will flower quite freely on the young wood a little later in the season.

LADY BETTY BALFOUR One of the finest late blue clematis, flowering during the months of September and October. Very large, deep blue, with an attractive centre of white stamens. This superb variety needs hard pruning every February and plenty of space should be allowed as during the summer it will cover twenty or thirty feet with ease. As it blooms late, a good sunny spot should be chosen.

LADY CAROLINE NEVILLE A lovely pale mauve with deeper bars down the centre of each sepal. Very large and sometimes semi-double flowers appear in May and June followed by true single, but smaller flowers, on the young wood during the summer. Belonging to the Lanuginosa group, Lady Caroline Neville needs little pruning and will grow to a height of up to twenty feet. A south or west aspect is best for this lovely lady.

LADY NORTHCLIFFE This well-known and popular variety has large deep-lavender-blue flowers from June until October, with an attractive centre of cream stamens which sets the flowers off most effectively. When first in bloom, the flowers have a purple shade which disappears after a few days. By the time they have been out for a week or more, they are almost a true-blue, fading to a bright metallic blue. A good variety for a small garden on a south or west wall, as it is not too vigorous, growing only to a height of about six feet and about three to four feet in width. Needs no pruning and flowers equally well on both the young and old wood,

LASURSTERN This superb variety flowers in May and June on the old wood, and occasionally one gets a repeat performance in September. These flowers are very large, often measure eight inches in diameter, and consist of six finely shaped large and pointed sepals. The colour is a deep purple-blue, and the contrasting mass of white stamens is very effective. A well-grown plant will bear up to a hundred or more of these enormous and exotic blooms, each individual flower lasting up to six weeks, gradually fading in the course of time to a light blue, but still remaining a good colour. Lasurstern needs no pruning, makes a plant of about six to ten feet in height and about the same distance across, and is a good variety for a south or west position.

LINCOLN STAR One of the newer striped varieties. The stripe in Lincoln Star, however, is so wide that it almost fills the whole sepal, giving the impression of a bright cochineal-pink flower edged with flesh-pink. The flowers are a good size, six to eight inches across, the sepals are long and pointed, six to eight in number, and the maroon centre of stamens makes it a handsome flower. Little pruning is necessary, as this variety belongs to the Patens group. May and June is the main flowering period, but one gets a generous repeat performance in August and September with flowers smaller but still of the same good colour. It makes a plant of up to twelve feet and is ideal for any aspect.

MADAME ÉDOUARD ANDRÉ . One of the best of the so-called reds. There are, of course, no real-red clematis, the colour being more maroon, but Madame Édouard André is the best all-round ' red ' variety for the amateur gardener and will grow in any aspect. The warm velvet-red flowers are produced in great profusion from early June until well into September. The flowers are about five to six inches across, a good round shape with six wide sepals, full and pointed. Like Comtesse de Bouchard, this variety does not attain great heights, and so is an excellent clematis for the low wall. The maximum height is about six feet, and it can be trained to the same width, making a very effective plant when in full bloom with its hundreds of wine-coloured flowers. Madame Édouard André belongs to the Jackmanii group, and needs hard pruning every February.

MADAME LE COULTRE One of the finest whites in cultivation. The enormous ' soup-plate ' flowers of eight or more sepals are fully nine inches in diameter, and the centre of yellow stamens helps to emphasise the whiteness of the flower. The flowers are produced on old and young wood with great freedom, and the first enormous blooms appear in June. Then as the young wood develops, the following month, we get a large number of smaller but equally beautiful flowers, descending in a snow-storm of bloom. The plant itself is very vigorous and strong, and will attain a height of thirty feet or more. It will also broaden out to six or eight feet as well, making a very fine specimen plant for a sunny position. This variety belongs to the Lanuginosa group and can be left unpruned. It flowers well on the young wood, though, and is often treated as a Jackmanii and cut down every February.

MISS BATEMAN This lovely white variety has been popular for over eighty years. The flowers are of medium size, about five to six inches in diameter, slightly fragrant, with six to eight wide sepals, so that the whole effect is of a good, well shaped bloom. They are pure white with a cream-coloured bar down the centre of each sepal, this bar fading with age so that the fully matured flowers are a pure white. The centre of the bloom is most attractive, the stamens being a chocolate-red surrounded by a corona of flesh-coloured filaments which makes a most effective contrast. This is a splendid variety for growing in any aspect, or for growing indoors. Most clematis resent being indoors, preferring plenty of air and light, but Miss Bateman grows well in a large pot or tub, flowers freely from May to September and needs little or no pruning. A very useful variety, and one of the shorter-growing varieties, six to eight feet being its maximum height.

MRS CHOLMONDELEY This is one of the longest-flowering clematis in existence. The flowering period is almost non-stop, from May until the end of September. The blooms are of a lavender-blue, and the sepals are long, narrow and separated, so that the individual flower lacks the fullness of other varieties in this group. However, this is amply rewarded by the mass of bloom it sends out during the course of the season ; hundreds of flowers are produced in a never-ending cascade of beauty. The growth of Mrs Cholmondeley is strong and vigorous, and a fully grown plant will attain a height of up to thirty feet. The first flowers to appear are very large, about nine inches in diameter, each long elliptic sepal being tipped with purple. The flowers that appear almost directly afterwards do not have this purple tip ; the general colour then is lighter in tone, and the flowers are smaller, but as there are so many this is hardly noticeable in the general colour effect. A good strong variety for any position in the garden, needing little or no pruning after the first year.

NELLY MOSER Almost everyone knows of Nelly Moser, one of the most popular varieties to have been introduced in the last fifty years. The huge eight- to nine-inch blooms are produced with amazing profusion, and I have seen plants with over three hundred blooms, many of them overlapping. The eight sepals are long, broad and pointed, making a very showy bloom. The colour is a pale pinkish-mauve with a broad band of deep carmine-red running down the centre of each sepal. A mass of long golden-brown stamens in the centre adds the final exotic touch to a most distinct and glorious bloom. Nelly Moser has one fault, however : it fades badly in full sun, and as its flowering time is May and June when the sun is growing rather fierce, we may soon lose the delicate colour and be left with a silvery-white flower. Still, this variety is so hardy and robust that we can grow it quite well on a north wall where it will retain its lovely colour. West or north-west walls are the ideal spots, as here the plant will get a certain amount of sun in late afternoon and evening when it has lost its midday power. Nelly Moser will eventually grow up to twelve feet or more, and attain a width of six to eight feet, and needs no pruning after the first year.

PERLE D'AZUR A lovely sky-blue, the only light-blue variety in the Jackmanii group. The flowers are about five to six inches in diameter, and they are produced very freely from June to September. The centre is a tuft of greenish stamens—a typical

Jackmanii habit—and the sepals are broad, four to six in number, rounded and ribbed. The plant will attain about fifteen feet in height and makes a wonderful show in the summer with its quite distinctive colour. It should be pruned hard every February. A good variety for any aspect.

PRINS HENDRIK This variety with its large azure-blue flowers is grown in Holland as a cut flower, a number of large greenhouses being devoted to its cultivation for this purpose. The normal flowering time of this magnificent variety is mid-summer, July and August, and it belongs to the Lanuginosa group and so needs little pruning. The sepals of Prince Hendrik are long and pointed, curving gracefully backwards with beautifully crenulated edges making it a flower of great distinction. A sunny spot is the best for this fine variety, which will make a plant of about twelve feet or more.

THE PRESIDENT The richness and depth of colour of this variety is remarkable, a deep royal purple, with a very long flowering period. The first eight-inch blooms appear on the old wood in June. After these flowers have finished, the young wood starts to grow, producing a good number of flowers in two or three bursts of blooming during the summer, right through to the end of September. The President is a beautifully shaped flower of eight pointed sepals with dark-purple stamens, a very handsome and valuable variety for the south wall as it does not fade in the hot sun. The President is rather slow-growing, needs no pruning and does not grow much over eight feet. It is well worth a place in the garden in any aspect except north.

VICTORIA This variety is unique amongst the Jackmanii varieties with its large six-sepalled flowers of a soft heliotrope-mauve. An ideal variety to grow on a shrub or small tree, it will flower during the whole summer with great freedom. Hard pruning is necessary as the blooms are produced on the young wood only, but it will cover up to twenty feet during the summer quite easily.

VILLE DE LYON A good late-flowering red. Its medium round flowers appear in late July and last until the end of October. This variety must have a south wall, or its later flowers will not get a chance to develop. The sepals of Ville de Lyon are broad and round, giving the flower a very full appearance. The colour of the lower part is a bright carmine with edges a much deeper red. The stamens are a bright golden, contrasting very effectively with the rest of the flower. This variety should be pruned hard every year for the best result, but if left unpruned it will produce a few much larger flowers on the old wood in May and June. One or two vines could be left every year to obtain these early flowers, cutting the rest of the plant right down in February. Ten to twelve feet is about the normal height of Ville de Lyon.

VYVYAN PENNELL The best double clematis, producing very large double flowers in May and June. The colour is deep violet-blue suffused with carmine and purple, with a centre of golden stamens—a magnificent flower. No pruning is necessary, as these exotic-looking blooms are produced on the old wood. Single flowers will appear on the young wood later in the summer. Vyvyan Pennell will make a plant of up to twelve feet in height, and with its mass of rosette-shaped flowers during the late spring and early summer, is a wonderful sight.

W. E. GLADSTONE Flowers of this famous variety often measure nine inches across. They are really enormous but, even so, extremely beautiful. The colour is a beautiful lilac-blue, with the white stamens and black anthers contrasting well with the satiny sepals. When fully out, W. E. Gladstone is a magnificent sight. The sepals are overlapping and very flat, the outer edges drooping downwards in a quite distinctive manner.

Flowering from June to August, it needs little pruning after the first year, and makes a plant of up to twelve feet high, preferring a south or west aspect.

WILLIAM KENNETT   A very fine variety.   It makes a splendid plant of up to twenty feet, covering a wide area in width as well. The individual blooms are about eight inches in diameter, and the eight sepals are very wide so that they overlap each other, making a full and beautifully shaped flower.   They are ribbed down the centre with three distinct ribs, with crenulated edges to the sepals. The colour is a good lavender-mauve with brown stamens, surrounded by masses of lighter-coloured filaments giving the appearance of a rosette.   This variety blooms at the height of the summer, is a great asset to any garden and needs little or no pruning, flowering mainly on the old wood in June and July.   A south or west aspect is best for this magnificent variety.

EIGHT : QUESTION-TIME WITH CLEMATIS

I HAVE been asked many questions about clematis during the several years' pleasure I have had growing these most rewarding climbers. How to plant, prune and train them are, of course, the main ones. These have, I hope, been answered in full in the early chapters of this book. A number of questions are asked, however, which do not fall under those three headings—some of them are rather unusual too. A selection of them is given in this chapter in the hope that some, at least, may answer the reader's own queries. They are not given in any special order.

' *Can clematis be grown in tubs ?* '

Yes, they can, and quite successfully too. The only snag is that they are likely to dry out unless constantly watered, and it is difficult to keep the roots shaded. If these two things can be arranged, there is no reason why they should not be a source of great pleasure on the terrace, in the hall or even as a house plant. When planting them in tubs, be sure to give them good drainage —broken pots or clinkers, and making certain that they have adequate drainage holes. If you can get some good manure, put this on the top of the drainage. Plant the clematis firmly in a good compost ; a John Innes will be very suitable, with a handful of bone-meal mixed in. The size of the tub is rather important, as clematis are deep-rooting plants, so the tub should be eighteen inches deep if possible, though a foot square will give the plant enough soil to last for several years. A mulching in the autumn of well-rotted manure and a handful of sulphate of potash in the spring will help to keep the plant going. A fortnightly feeding of liquid manure is also very beneficial during the growing season, but this should not be given during the flowering season, as it makes the flowers finish rather quickly. Keeping the roots cool can be achieved by planting small bedding plants round the base of the clematis, or by standing the tub behind something that shades it, until the plant makes enough top growth to do its own shading, or by filling the top of the tub with pebbles.

' *My clematis is quite out of hand, very untidy, a large flower, but I do not know which variety. How do I prune it ?* '

The best thing to do in this case is to cut the plant right down in February, and start afresh from the bottom. If a thick main stem has developed, with no shoots for a few feet, then this old stem must not be cut. Only trim down to the bottom buds of each shoot that breaks from the main stem. This still leaves the base of the plant bare, so one way of dealing with this is to layer a shoot in front of the base of the stem ; that is, if a shoot can be disentangled from the thick mass that sometimes develops. Layering a shoot like this will give your plant a new lease of life, as once the layer has rooted, it will form a strong new plant, which can be trained to cover the base of the old plant. Cutting your plant back drastically like this will do it the world of good, and you should get some strong new shoots which can be trained properly.

How to tell whether your plant is one that needs annual pruning or not ? The plant will bloom on the young wood whichever variety, as most clematis will, and if it blooms profusely from July to October then it is one of the Jackmanii types that needs pruning hard every February ; but if it blooms only moderately, then it is probably a Patens type and should not be pruned. The following spring and early summer will confirm if it belongs to this group, as you will have a fine show of enormous flowers.

' I have a cold north wall ; will any varieties grow there ? '

There are several good clematis for clothing a north wall, which will give you a mass of flower in this unpromising position. The best, of course, are in the rampant Montana section, those spring and early-summer mountain clematis wreathed in masses of white and various shades of pink flowers ; *C. spooneri* and *C. spooneri rosea* are also excellent varieties, white and a lovely apple-blossom pink ; also the soft pink of the ' Hairy Clematis ', *C. chrysocoma*. Two more strong and vigorous growers in this section are *C. vedrariensis rosea*, sweetly scented, pale pink, and *C. vedrariensis* ' Highdown ', double the size and a deeper colour. These all need plenty of space, for they grow up to twenty to thirty feet in a year.

For the smaller wall the clear mountain blue of *C. alpina* is ideal ; with its nodding flowers in April and May, it is a splendid variety for a six-foot space. The wine-coloured *C. alpina* ' Ruby ' is also good, and the double white *C. alpina* ' White Moth '. *C. macropetala* is also an essential for the north wall, with its double blue nodding flowers of great beauty, and there is the mauve-pink variety *C. macropetala* ' *Markhamii* ', both flowering in April and May.

These are all the small-flowering varieties, but there are several of the large-flowering hybrids that will do very well on a north wall. ' Nelly Moser ' is especially good, as it keeps its colour so well in the shade, and several of the striped ones are useful. ' Barbara Jackman ', a beautiful petunia-mauve with a crimson bar down the centre of each sepal, is good, and so is ' Lincoln Star ', a cochineal-pink with a maroon centre. ' Bee's Jubilee ', similar to ' Nelly Moser ' but a better colour, and

' Barbara Dibley ', another striped one with lovely long pointed sepals, are both ideal for large-flowering north-wall varieties. They are all spring-and-early-summer-flowering varieties. Some of the Jackmanii varieties are useful too ; they will flower during summer and right through until the late autumn when planted on a north wall, as this delays their flowering period for a few weeks. ' Jackmanii ', the lovely old purple, is ideal and gives a tremendous show on a shady wall. The rose-pink ' Comtesse de Bouchard ' is also very good, and they look very well planted together with their pink and purple flowers intermingled. ' Hagley Hybrid ' also does well on north walls, and the velvet-red ' Madame Édouard André '.

' *Are clematis any good as cut flowers ?* '

Yes, they are, and the surprising thing is that very few people use them in floral decoration. Large-flowering varieties will last up to three weeks in water. The very large varieties may be *too* big for this purpose, but even one bloom in a tall slender vase in the Japanese manner looks most effective. Some people abhor the idea of floating flowers, but I think that clematis are ideally suited to this method. One enormous bloom floating in the centre of a shallow black bowl, surrounded by some suitable foliage (not clematis foliage), makes a charming display for the hall table, or even the dining-table—without the drawback of hiding the guests ! The small-flowering species are also ideal for the big display ; their trailing sprays of dainty flowers can be used to great effect. Cut the blooms early in the morning if possible, and bruise the ends of the stems to make them last in water, or dip them in boiling water for a few seconds.

If a flower droops after being arranged, place it overnight in a bucket of water, so that the bloom is floating. By the morning it will have stiffened up again. If this can be done before arranging, so that the stem has had a long drink, so much the better, for it will then last much longer in water. The seed heads of clematis are used more than the flowers, I fancy. One often sees at harvest festivals that generous use is made of the wild variety *C. vitalba*, the ' Old Man's Beard ' or ' Traveller's Joy '. There are other varieties having useful seed heads, besides our hedgerow native. *C. flammula* is useful, and also *C. tangutica*, and some of the seed heads produced by the large-flowering hybrids are quite magnificent. ' Henryii ' and ' Nelly Moser ' are two varieties that produce natural ' whirligig ' masterpieces.

' *My " Ernest Markham " grows like a weed but never flowers ; how can I make it bloom ?* '

This variety is a very strong-growing clematis and sometimes has this habit of making a good deal of wood but producing very few flowers. The way to encourage this lovely bright-red variety to give a good show is to nip out the tips of the shoots when it reaches a height of six feet or more. This should be done in July, and will encourage the shoots to branch out and produce flowering wood. One or two other varieties have this annoying habit, but stopping the shoots when they have almost fully developed will cure this blindness, giving you a fine show of bloom. ' Ernest Markham ' sometimes flowers on the old wood in May and June if left unpruned ; but as it is such a late-flowering treasure, hard pruning of this variety is best.

' *How long does the average plant live ?* '

Clematis are very long-living plants, and there are records of them living for over seventy years. In the Montana group are, I think, the varieties that survive the longest. On some of our big country houses there are plants that must be a hundred years old. They have enormous trunks, as thick as one's arm, and cover an extensive area. The Jackmanii varieties are also long-living and may exceed fifty years with ease. For most varieties I should imagine that twenty-five years would be a good average. Clematis have only been popular for the last hundred years, so they may be even longer-living than we think.

' *How do I prune my* C. montana *which has got into a terrible tangle ?* '

There are two ways in which these early-flowering varieties can be pruned. One is in February, when the plant can be cut back quite hard, almost to the old thick stems, but not actually cutting into them, as buds are not quite so freely produced from this old wood. With this method, however, all the spring flowers will be lost. The second and best method is to wait until one has had the flowers ; then, immediately after flowering, cut back as hard as possible. This is the growing time for C. *montana*, so the new shoots will appear almost immediately. A good mulching should be given in the spring and a handful of sulphate of potash, and the plant will soon send out masses of strong shoots that will be next year's flowering wood. They can then be trained correctly.

' *Should I remove the seed heads after flowering ?* '

This is not really necessary, especially with the small-flowering species, but when young plants of the large-flowering varieties produce one or two flowers soon after planting, followed by an enormous seed head, these could be removed before they develop. The energy of the plant will then be transferred to the producing of new shoots. Once the plant is established there will be no need to remove seed heads, as these are decorative and very useful for floral arrangements.

' *Are there evergreen clematis ?* '

Yes, there are three evergreen varieties that are hardy in this country ; there are several others, but most of them need the protection of a cool greenhouse. The three varieties are *C. armandii*, *C. calycina* and *C. cirrhosa*. They all flower very early in the year, *C. calycina* and *C. cirrhosa* blooming in the mild spells of the winter, with dainty bell-shaped flowers and graceful fern-like evergreen foliage, glistening and glossy green. *C. armandii* has much larger leaves, about eight inches long. This is a very handsome variety which, even when not in flower, is very decorative. The flowers are small and ' montana-like ', and are produced in masses during April and May. This is quite hardy round our coasts, but inland should have the protection of a warm south wall.

' *Why do some varieties bloom only at the top ?* '

These are the Jackmanii and Viticella groups, which flower on the young wood only. This takes a couple of months or so to produce, so we cut these varieties right down in the early spring. The flowers are produced on the ends of these shoots, so it is only natural for these varieties to have their flowers at the top. With a little bit of careful training this can be avoided, however. When your plant is well established and has four or more shoots coming from the base, prune hard in February as usual. Let the shoots grow naturally up the wall or trellis to about three or four feet, then stop half of them by nipping out the growing tips. This will encourage them to break, producing flowering wood lower down the plant, thus clothing the some-times bare and unsightly base of the plant.

' *Why does my plant look dead at the bottom but alive at the top* '

This question is connected with the previous one, for the leaves of the plant will naturally die off at the base before the younger ones above. Plenty of moisture and feeding, however, will help to keep the lower leaves looking green for a much longer period. ' Ville de Lyon ' is a variety that is very prone to this dead-looking base. Planting something tall in front— delphiniums, for instance—will hide the failing of this lovely red variety, but stopping half the plant is the best method.

' I want a succession of flowers from May to October in as many colours as possible, large- and small-flowering. Which twelve varieties would you recommend ? '

Variety	Flowering period	Colour	Large- or small-flowering
C. *montana rubens*	May–June	Pink	Small
' Nelly Moser '	May–June	Mauve-pink, with carmine stripes	Large
C. *spooneri*	May–June	White	Small
' Mrs Cholmondeley '	May–Sept.	Lavender-blue	Large
' Henryi '	June–Sept.	White	Large
' William Kennett '	June–Aug.	Lavender	Large
C. *viticella rubra*	July–Sept.	Red	Small
' Jackmanii '	July–Sept.	Purple	Large
' Comtesse de Bouchard '	July–Sept.	Pink	Large
Ernest Markham	July–Oct.	Red	Large
C. *tangutica*	Aug.–Oct.	Yellow	Small
C. *flammula*	Aug.–Oct.	White	Small

' Are there any scented clematis ? '

Only a few varieties, mostly the small-flowering species. The only large-flowering variety to have any real scent is ' Fair Rosamund ', similar in colour to ' Nelly Moser ', which has a delicate primrose-violet fragrance. ' Duchess of Edinburgh ', the double white, is reported to have a scent, but this is very faint. ' Barbara Jackman ' has quite a delicate fragrance, also ' Sealand Gem ', a heliotrope in colour. C. *armandii*, the white evergreen, has a sweet scent, so has the early-flowering *C. montana* ' Elizabeth ', with its pale-pink flowers ; its vanilla fragrance fills the air, especially after a shower. *C. vedrariensis rosea*, similar to *C. montana* ' Elizabeth ', is also very fragrant. *C. flammula*, the ' Fragrant Virgin's Bower ', is well named, the tiny white flowers having a rich scent in the late-summer and autumn garden. At this time we have the cowslip-scented *C. rehderiana*, with a delightful fragrance which at this time of the year reminds us of the spring. A semi-herbaceous variety, giving off a rich hawthorn perfume, is *C. coerulea odorata*, which has small reddish-purple flowers. The herbaceous varieties *C. davidiana* and *C. jouiniana campanile* are also sweetly scented.

' Will clematis grow in the north of Scotland ? '

Certainly. They are very hardy plants, much hardier than their fragile appearance suggests. They thrive and flower profusely in Norway and Sweden, so they are quite happy anywhere n the British Isles.

' May I plant two different varieties together ? '

Yes, you can, but it is advisable to plant two of the same pruning habits, otherwise you will run into trouble when it comes to pruning. Two early-flowering varieties like ' Nelly Moser ', mauve-pink striped, and ' Mrs Cholmondeley ', lavender, which do not need pruning, can be planted in the same spot. These two colours go well together. ' Mrs Cholmondeley ' will flower throughout the summer, and ' Nelly Moser ' will give a second blooming period in August and September. ' Jackmanii ' (purple) and ' Comtesse de Bouchard ' (pink) are also another good pair for summer flowering : these are two varieties that should be cut down every year. Another good combination for late blooming is ' Ernest Markham ' (red) and ' Gipsy Queen ' (purple), two hard-pruning varieties. For spring flowering, the pink and white C. *montana* can be planted together with great effect, also the pink and blue C. *macropetala*. The purple and red C. *viticella* make a fine late-summer and autumn contrast. They can also be planted with the yellow C. *tangutica*,

' *How far apart should clematis be planted ?* '

This depends on the varieties. The rampant species need a good space to grow in, but some of the smaller varieties can be planted quite close together. If you are growing two for mixing the colour, they can be planted about a foot apart, but if each variety is to develop to its normal area, then they should be planted about six feet apart.

' *My flowers have come out green this year. Why is this ?* '

Fortunately this only rarely occurs, and seems to be related to the previous summer and winter. If we get a wet dull summer, then the wood does not ripen properly, and if this is followed by a very mild winter the first flowers to appear will be green, or have a greenish tinge to them. This happens, particularly to ' Barbara Dibley ', ' Nelly Moser ' and ' Mrs Cholmondeley '. A good dressing of sulphate of potash in the very early spring will correct this fault and give the flowers a good colour.

' *Are there any varieties that will grow indoors ?* '

Clematis are not very good as house plants. They like the open air and natural growing conditions. But there is one variety that will tolerate the indoor atmosphere, and this is the white ' Miss Bateman '. It is a medium star-shaped flower and has a chocolate-red centre, making it a very attractive free-flowering plant. This does not need pruning and will make a fine pot plant grown on a wire frame. The pink ' Comtesse de

Bouchard ' is another good variety for growing indoors. If the plant can have a certain amount of time outdoors, so much the better ; after the flowering has finished and until the spring is the ideal period for resting.

' *I have a small walled-in town garden, with a six-foot-high wall. Which varieties should I plant ?* '

There are quite a few free-flowering clematis that do not take up too much room and the following varieties would do well in a small garden :

Variety	Flowering period	Colour	Large- or small-flowering
C. *alpina*	April–May	Blue	Small
C. *macropetala*	April–May	Blue	Small
' Barbara Jackman '	May & June	Petunia-mauve with crimson bar	Large
' Barbara Dibley '	May & June	Pansy-violet with deep bar	Large
' The President '	May–Sept.	Purple	Large
' Miss Bateman '	June–Sept.	White	Large
' Lady Northcliffe '	June–Sept.	Blue	Large
' Hagley Hybrid '	June–Sept.	Shell-pink	Large
' Comtesse de Bouchard '	June–Sept.	Pink	Large
' Madame Édouard André '	June–Sept.	Red	Large

' *Can I move my clematis ? They are about six years old.*'

Clematis don't like being moved, but providing it is done at the correct time of the year—that is, late autumn—then it can be successfully accomplished. When the plant has finished flowering and growing, cut it back quite hard, so that it is easy to dig up. Prepare the new site first of all, by digging a fairly deep and wide hole, and making sure of good drainage at the bottom with some good manure there as well. Your plant will have made quite a lot of roots in five or six years. These do not spread out very far, so there will be no need to dig very widely round the plant, but you will have to dig quite deeply to get all the roots without breaking too many. When replanting, tread the soil very firmly round the plant, and in the spring make sure it has not been loosened by frosts. During the first year after moving, keep the plant well watered until it has become settled in its new spot. It will sometimes sulk for the first season until it has re-established itself, but after that all will be well.

' *Are grafted plants more liable to wilt than plants on their own roots ?* '

Although the general opinion is that grafted plants are more liable to wilt than those on their own roots, there is no justification for this statement. I have known plants raised from cuttings collapse as well as plants that have been grafted. No hard pruning during the first year had been carried out though, and I am sure that this is the answer to Clematis Wilt : prune hard and often during the first year. Most nurseries nowadays grow their plants from cuttings, but several varieties are rather difficult to strike, and so some grafting is necessary. All grafted clematis eventually get on their own roots, as when they are potted into a larger-sized pot they are planted with the union below the soil. This encourages the graft to send out roots above the union, and within a year or two it is on its own roots, the stock being discarded and disappearing in time.

NINE : PROPAGATING CLEMATIS

LAYERING is an excellent way of increasing clematis, and really it is the best method of all. For the amateur it is the easiest and safest way, and there is no need for greenhouses, frames or heat. Once the operation has been completed, the layers can be left undisturbed until the following year. One needs a well-developed plant, however, one that has some good strong vines growing from the base of the plant. Those varieties that are cut down almost to the ground each February will give us ideal wood for layering. August is the best time for this operation.

First of all we prepare some special soil, possibly John Innes Compost, and a few five-inch pots, one for each vine. We then gently disentangle our vines, bringing them down on to the soil. At the spot where they can be bent down to touch the soil without undue strain, we sink one of our pots filled with the special compost to a little below the ground level. The vine is then twisted to break the bark at the spot where it is to be pegged into the soil, or a cut is made lengthwise either at a node or in between the nodes, and dusted with a hormone powder. The twist or cut is pegged firmly into the pots filled with special soil, covered with garden soil, and a stone is placed on top as an extra precaution. The whole area must be kept moist during hot weather. As many vines as there are on the plant can be treated in this way, and the layers left where they are until the following autumn, twelve months later. This may seem a long time to wait, but it is well worth it, as we shall find a pot sometimes bursting with roots, and a strong healthy plant which can be severed from its parent and planted in its new position.

Cuttings are the next best method, and these are taken in quite an unusual manner. When cuttings of other plants are made, they normally have a heel of the old wood, or are made of lengths cut close below a joint. In clematis, however, we cut them in between the joints or nodes, so they are called internodal cuttings. These are best taken in the early summer, May or June being the most suitable time. If we can take plants in pots into a warm greenhouse in March we shall get some fine wood for cutting by May. Cuttings taken from plants outside are almost as good, and will root well. Semi-hard wood is the best, the soft tips of the stems and the bottom hard wood being quite useless. So from a four-foot vine we shall only use the centre foot or so. Cuttings can be made from each joint or node, and as clematis joints are often so far apart, this is the most practical way, as with a node at the top and one at the bottom the length of the cutting is unmanageable. Cut half-way in between the joints, then, and we shall have three or four cuttings from each length. The stem above the nodes should be trimmed as closely as possible to the joints, making sure that both top and bottom cuts are clean. Leaves on clematis cuttings are a nuisance, as they are so large and twisted, but we can remove one of them without doing any damage. Our cuttings are now ready and can be inserted in a pot of sharp sand or any suitable striking medium. Make sure the pot has good drainage and that it is always kept moist. These pots should be placed inside a propagating frame in the greenhouse, and if some bottom heat is available so much the better, but they will root in a cool greenhouse. They will need very little attention for the first fortnight. If they are kept moist and shaded when the sun is out, they will be all right. After two or three weeks we must watch out for dead or mildewed leaves, and these should be removed immediately before the disease spreads. A month or six weeks will see the cuttings well rooted, and they can then be potted into individual pots in a John Innes Compost, but still kept ' close ' in the propagating frame until they are safely established. Then air can be given in increasing amounts until, by August, they are put outside in a cold frame, there to spend the winter. In the following spring they are potted-on into the larger pots into a stiffer medium, and kept in a cool house for a few weeks. They are staked with canes during this period, then planted in their permanent spots or plunged out in the garden ; that is, the plant in its pot is buried in the garden until the autumn, when it can be planted.

Grafting is another method, used mainly by nurserymen, but one that the amateur with a greenhouse could amuse himself with. Clematis are grafted on the native variety of this country, C. *vitalba*, or the southern European variety C. *viticella*. Many people frown on this method, but as grafted plants, when potted-on, are always potted with the union below the soil level, the scion has a chance to produce its own roots. One certainly gets a well-grown plant much more quickly by grafting than by any other method, provided one has the stocks on which to graft. These must be raised from seed, and they must be two years old before they are big enough for grafting.

Wood for the scions has to be obtained by forcing plants in the greenhouse. Potted plants are brought into a heated greenhouse in December, and by February, when they have made three feet of nice new growth, they are ready for grafting. The stocks, which should have been slightly forced in a cold frame, are then brought in. Armed with a very sharp budding-knife and some short lengths of raffia, we are now ready for the operation. The young growths from our forced plants are cut off low down and cut into sections, with one pair of leaves to each portion. The top growth of the stock is cut off and a good straight neck

71

of root is selected for grafting. A straight clean cut about half an inch long, just paring off the bark, is then made along the side of the stem ready to receive the scion. This is prepared by cutting down through the shoot of our named variety in between the pair of leaves, giving us two scions. When making this cut down in between the buds, the knife is brought out towards the thumb, a tricky operation, but ensuring that the scion will fit the cut on the stock. The two are then brought together, making sure that the bark on both scion and stock joins all the way down, for it is here that the union takes place, just inside the bark. Failure to fit the two pieces together means failure to grow.

Suitable lengths of raffia, about six inches long, should be moistened and split into thin lengths, for with this delicate operation a thin piece of raffia is essential. Holding the scion and stock firmly together, wind the raffia from top to bottom, firmly but gently, starting with about two turns above the leaf. At the bottom of the union, take a turn round the thumb with the raffia, making a half-hitch where the end of the raffia is passed through, and pull tight, securing the whole union. The top of the graft is then trimmed with a sharp knife, and the raffia at the bottom cut close to the binding.

The plants are then ready for potting. This is done as soon as possible after the grafting has been completed. Small ' 60s ' are usually the size required, and the plants potted in a John Innes Compost. They are then placed in the propagating frame with bottom heat in the greenhouse, where a temperature of at least 60° F. must be maintained. Left here for about three weeks they will need little attention beyond being kept moist and removing any dead leaves. After about three weeks the small bud at the bottom of the stem will start to swell. When the plants have grown half an inch they can be taken from the propagating frame and placed on the bench. Take care to shade them when the sun is shining, as they are very delicate at this period. When these plants are about three or four inches high, a small stick to support them is necessary, and as soon as they reach about nine or ten inches high, it is a good idea to ' stop ' them to encourage the plant to throw out a couple of shoots instead of just the one.

The young plants can now be moved into a cooler greenhouse. Clematis are very hardy things and do not like artificial heat. Potting-on time is now at hand, and larger pots, five- or six-inch, are necessary for this final move. A good compost should be used, and make sure that the union is well below the soil level. This will ensure that the scion will root and that eventually the plant will be on its own roots. From this time onwards there is little to do except keep the plant well watered and to provide a longer stake or cane. About June or July it will be sturdy enough to be planted outside or plunged in the garden until planting time in the autumn. Young plants often flower quite freely during their first year, but this will not hurt them. An occasional nipping-out of growing tips is a good thing, as this will help to make the plant more bushy and healthy.

Seed is the final method of propagation—perhaps the most exciting, but also the least reliable. True species come true from seed fairly well, but the varieties of species do not, neither do the large-flowering hybrids.

Seeds should be gathered in the autumn or as soon as ripe, and stored in a dry cool place during the winter. In the early spring they can be sown in a John Innes Seed Compost in seed pans, or pots ; they can also be sown directly they are gathered and wintered in a cold frame. The larger seed should be sown fairly deeply, but the small varieties, such as C. *tangutica*, will only just need covering. The fluffy seed heads are a little trouble-some, but with the large-flowering hybrids one could easily dibble them in, leaving the ' tail ' above the soil. Species will germinate quickly and will soon need pricking-out or potting-on, but large-flowering hybrids are not so quick to germinate. Sometimes they are up to three years before putting in an appearance, so never throw away seed pans if nothing appears. If after a couple of months there are no seedlings visible, put the seed pans outside in a cool frame or in a sheltered spot, and leave them there until the following spring. Bring them in to the warm greenhouse, and if nothing appears again, repeat the outdoor treatment. One often gets one or two germinating each time. They must be carefully lifted out of the pan without disturbing the other dormant seeds. These little seedlings should be carefully potted into small pots and then, as they grow, into larger pots, until eventually they flower, usually about three years after germination. Nine times out of ten, when this occurs, the result is very disappointing, but there is always that tenth time which may result in a new colour, or a wilt-resisting plant—and fame for the raiser if he or she decides to name it after themselves.

TEN : HYBRIDISING

THIS is a very interesting task, and although we shall be getting very many failures, there is always the chance that a rare new variety may be raised. What a thrill to see a new flower opening, and to realise that for the very first time in the history of clematis one has achieved a fresh colour or combination of colours ! Think of the excitement there must have been when ' Nelly Moser ' first opened its sepals many years ago. The raisers must have known immediately that they had a winner.

The method of hybridising is very simple : the pollen of one variety is transferred to the stigma of another, bees and other insects are kept away, and when the seed has ripened, it is sown. Three to six years later we may be gazing at a fabulous new variety that will sweep the clematis world.

This transferring of the pollen must be done at just the right time, of course, and it is best to do a little preparation beforehand. The flower we select to be the seed-bearing plant should be just on the point of opening from the bud. All the sepals (which take the place of petals in clematis) must be carefully cut off with a small pair of scissors to reveal the anthers and stigma. To prevent any self-pollination, the anthers must also be cut off. The stigma, which is the central tuft of silky bodies in the centre of the flower, is left to await the time when it is ready for receiving pollen from another variety. A small muslin bag should be placed over the stigma, tying it round the stem below the flower to prevent any pollen settling on the stigma from bees or by chance. The stigma is ready when the flower would normally be in full flower, which will be a few days after the sepals have been cut off in the bud stage. The best time to perform the operation of dusting the pollen is on a sunny day, in the morning if possible. The pollen from the desired cross is brought to the parent plant, and dusted on to the stigma either by gently shaking the pollen flower on to the other, or by collecting the pollen with a small paint-brush. This operation could be repeated in two or three days' time, just to make sure that fertilisation has taken place. Directly this operation has been completed, the muslin bag should be replaced and left in this position for a few days. When all danger of a chance cross has passed, remove the muslin bag, leaving the plant to nature's course to produce the seed. This will take some time, and it will be several weeks before the seed is ripe and fit for gathering. It can either be sown immediately, or kept until the spring and sown in gentle heat. Germination may be slow, so if nothing appears the first year do not despair : often two years or even more may elapse beore the seedlings appear, and then it will be another three years before they flower. So hybridising is a very slow job with clematis, and after all this time we may have nothing worth while to show for our trouble ! On the other hand we *may*. . . . Records of the crosses one makes should always be kept and the parentage recorded.

There are, of course, many lovely varieties today, and I think it will have to be a very outstanding new variety to make much of an impression. Yellow is the only colour that is missing in the large-flowering hybrid, but few people want to see a large yellow clematis : like the pink daffodil, it would never be really popular. A wilt-resisting strain of clematis would, of course, be something much more exciting. Perhaps one day we shall be able to evolve a race of wilt-resisting plants. Our gardens would then soon fill with this most graceful and beautiful climber.

ELEVEN : CLEMATIS HISTORY

THE only clematis known in this country before the sixteenth century was the native *C. vitalba*, the ' Traveller's Joy ' or ' Old Man's Beard ' of our hedgerows. This rampant variety is known by many other names in different parts of the country, including ' Old Man's Woozard ', ' Grandfather's Whiskers ', ' Hedge Feathers ' and ' Snow in Harvest ', to name but a few. The stems have also been used for smoking, which has earned it the names of ' Smoking Cane ', ' Boys' Bacca ' and ' Shepherd's Delight '. *C. vitalba* has coarse foliage, and a small greeny-white flower produced in July and August which develops into a foam of highly decorative seed heads in the autumn. The rope-like branches will cover small trees, and in the chalky parts of the country give an almost jungle-like effect to our woodlands.

In 1596 the dainty *C. viticella*, with its purple saucer-shaped flowers, was introduced to this country. The name of ' Virgin's Bower ' is thought by some to be a tribute to the virgin Queen Elizabeth I, but others think that it is much older and is, in fact, in honour of the Virgin Mary. Another popular name which supports this theory is ' Ladies' Bower ', a tribute to Our Lady ; also the couplet, ' When Mary left us here below, the Virgin's Bower began to blow '. The wild clematis is in flower, of course, at the time of the Feast of the Assumption in August.

As the famous sailors of the Elizabethan era brought home rare and unusual plants, other species began to appear in our gardens. *C. flammula*, *C. cirrhosa* and *C. integrifolia* were the first of many species to arrive in England. By the end of the eighteenth century a large number of small-flowering varieties had been added to the collection from many different parts of the world.

Most varieties come from the temperate regions of the world —clematis in the tropics are very rare. The most prolific region of all is China, and it was from this country that the large-flowering variety *C. lanuginosa* was first introduced by Robert Fortune early in the nineteenth century. About the same time *C. patens* arrived from Japan, as another large-flowering species. Then the nurserymen of the day began to get busy, and new varieties came thick and fast.

The first hybrid appeared in 1835 at Henderson's Nursery in St John's Wood, London, and was called ' Hendersonii '. This variety is a cross between *C. integrifolia* and *C. viticella* and has the leaves of the former variety with viticella-like flowers. It is still available, but now goes under the name of *C. eriostemon*.

C. Noble of Sunningdale, Messrs Crisps & Sons of Tunbridge Wells and Messrs G. Baker & Son of Bagshot are three more of the early famous names in the clematis world, and between them they raised varieties still to be found today : ' Miss Bateman ', ' Lady Londesborough ', ' Countess of Lovelace ' and ' Fair Rosamund ', to name but a few. Many varieties raised from 1850 to the end of the century have disappeared from our gardens. They were mainly poor in colour and have been superseded by the modern varieties of today. Clematis are long-living plants, however, and there may still be varieties that were raised a hundred years or so ago, flourishing unknown in someone's garden.

Other nurseries engaged in hybridisation at this time were those of Isaac Anderson-Henry of Edinburgh, who gave us the still-famous large white ' Henryi ', and George Jackman and Son of Woking, whose name will forever be linked with clematis. Their famous ' Jackmanii ', sown in 1858, was the result of the crossing of *C. lanuginosa* with *C. hendersonii* and *C. viticella atrorubens*,

and it flowered first in 1862, and it is to celebrate the centenary
of the first flowering of the most famous and best loved of all
clematis that this book is published.

One hundred years ago clematis were new, but fast becoming
a favourite flower. Now in 1962 they are enjoying a welcome
return to public favour ; so long may the ' Queen of Climbers '
reign to fill our gardens throughout the live-long spring, summer
and autumn with their magnificent flowers, their diverse forms
and their great beauty.

INDEX

81

INDEX

Printed in Great Britain by
Thomas Nelson (Printers) Ltd, London and Edinburgh